*See back map for
locations to eat, drink,
shop and more

HOBART CITY

ELIZABETH STREET

PATRICK STREET

MURRAY STREET

HARRINGTON STREET

BRISBANE STREET

MELVILLE STREET

ARGYLE STREET

CAMPBELL STREET

ELIZABETH STREET

BATHURST STREET

CRITERION ST

MURRAY STREET

LIVERPOOL STREET

WATCHORN ST

HARRINGTON STREET

COLLINS STREET

MACQUARIE STREET

DAVEY STREET

MORRISON STREET

FRANKLIN WHARF

EVANS STREET

HUNTER STREET

MELVILLE STREET

BATHURST STREET

BARRACK STREET

MOLLE STREET

LIVERPOOL STREET

COLLINS STREET

MACQUARIE STREET

DAVEY STREET

SANDY BAY ROAD

GLADSTONE STREET

MONTPELIER RETREAT

JAMES ST

CASTRAY ESPLANADE

SALAMANCA PLACE

RUNNYMEDE STREET

KELLY STREET

SOUTH STREET

HAMPDEN ROAD

WATERLOO CRESCENT

FRANCIS ST

CROMWELL STREET

COLVILLE STREET

MARIEVILLE ESPLANADE

SANDY BAY ROAD

QUEEN STREET

SOUTHERN

9

B110

A10

11

B31

A3

RICHMOND

B62

7

5

NEW NORFOLK

MARIA ISLAND

3

1

4

2

HOBART

A9

B64

A6

6

10

8

TASMAN PENINSULA

**BRUNY
ISLAND**

Where we are

In this book we cover mainly south and south-east Tasmania. There are a few key hot spots we want to point out so you can get your bearings. Use these handy maps as a guide to planning where you'd like to venture.

❶ HOBART CITY

Recent times have shown a renewed passion for the CBD, with new eateries and businesses breathing life into laneways and main streets. Find yourself a hotdog underground, wander upstairs into a quaint cocktail bar or tuck into a fresh cray at a dining table overlooking the salty pots.

❷ SALAMANCA + BATTERY POINT

Here you'll find plenty of vibrant activity. Grand sandstone warehouses are now filled with stylish wine bars, artist studios, and boutique galleries. This is where Sydney to Hobart yachts come to dock, and it's home to Australia's largest outdoor market, Salamanca Market.

❸ NORTH HOBART

The NoHo strip has a great little buzz to it. Here you'll be spoilt for choice, with restaurants of various cuisines all neatly packed into a streetscape that also boasts the State Cinema, stylish homewares, salons, live music and more.

❹ KUNANYI/MOUNT WELLINGTON AREA

We're so blessed to have a mountain looking over us – the ideal wilderness backdrop for mountain biking or a leisurely wander up to The Springs. In just a short drive you can be up to your ankles in snow or meeting the local wildlife.

❺ DERWENT VALLEY

Full of surprises, this touring route is ideal for anyone who has a penchant for antiques, loves a brew (in the middle of a paddock) and appreciates fine wine. And we haven't even mentioned the acclaimed Agrarian Kitchen cooking school or the highland cattle.

❻ HUON VALLEY

If you like the idea of rolling green hills, rosy red apples and roadside stalls, head for the Huon. You'll find authentic farm gate friendliness and people who are proud of their Tassie patch. Fresh produce, folky singers, chilled cider, rustic sheds and cool-climate wine blend seamlessly in these parts.

❼ COAL RIVER VALLEY

Take the Coal River Valley trip and you'll be driving along a country road dotted with some of the island's finest vineyards. Stop in for a long lazy lunch at one of these, then make your way on to Richmond.

❽ CHANNEL + BRUNY

There's a reason why whole books have been devoted to Bruny, and the Channel is the type of region that instils calm. Explore Woodbridge and continue far down the Channel or hop across to Bruny for freshly shucked oysters, cheese, great walks and empty white beaches.

❾ HERITAGE HIGHWAY + HIGHLANDS

This part of Tassie breathes history. Take a few side roads and you'll come across the only man in the country producing 100 per cent rye whisky using bio-fuel, as well as Australia's oldest golf course and some of the best trout fishing around. Yes, you could drive straight through, but the treasures are found when you pull back a gear.

❿ TASMAN PENINSULA + PORT ARTHUR

Spectacular in every way, not only does the Tasman Peninsula have Port Arthur Historic Site as its world-renowned icon but the coastal rock formations and quirky towns en route mean this peninsula deserves far more than a day trip. Take your time on this one – you'll be glad you stopped in at Lime Bay and other hidden spots.

⓫ EAST COAST

There's a reason that Wineglass Bay consistently rates among the best beaches on the planet. And although the road to the east coast could host a Ferrari advertisement as it hugs the coastline, it doesn't like to boast. It's unpretentious and staggeringly beautiful.

ABOUT
Tasmania

Tasmania is a beautiful island tucked away at the bottom of the world, a secret many have yet to discover. Where else in the world can you say you've breathed the freshest air on earth, spotted a Tasmanian devil, plucked an oyster straight from the water, rafted down one of the world's last wild rivers, visited Australia's largest privately owned museum and met plenty of friendly faces along the way? We could go on ... There are more than 1000 mountains to climb, four distinctly fantastic seasons, UNESCO world heritage sites, cosy cafés, world-class resorts and wine that turns the heads of Frenchmen – all nestled into a place about the size of West Virginia or Ireland. And we want to help you discover our Tasmania.

How to use the book

The book is easy to follow. It's divided into regions, beginning with local tips and moving into itineraries, snappy features and listings of where to eat, drink, shop, play and stay. You'll find snippets direct from locals who live here. Your journey begins in central Hobart and moves out to other regions with a handy map to show you the way. You'll find recipes that aren't your standard cup of flour. Courtesy of the blog *Island Menu*, you'll be taken on an adventure from the ocean to the plate.

Also tucked in here are itineraries so you can enjoy Tassie the way we locals do, and a collection of stories on our makers, those who provide the creative pulse to this place.

At the back of the book is your water-resistant map. It's packed full of information on where to eat and drink, shop and play in the Hobart area. It'll be your perfect mate for days you don't want to carry the book and you'd like a quick snapshot of things on offer. Happy exploring.

About the book

I love my home – so I'm thrilled you have this book in your hands. I've carefully handpicked all that makes Tassie special and packed these pages full of local secrets.

What inspired this book? At my Salamanca stall each Saturday I meet lovely folk who have ventured to the world's edge and ask me what to do while they're here. I often suggest a café or a favourite day trip but wish I could share more of what we locals know and love. So I got busy writing.

Whether you're a local or passing through, I want you to know where to find a great wine bar for a girls' weekend, or where to cast a line, or how to find those little-known cafés you'll never want to leave. Much of this book is southern-focused (aside from some feature stories) but untapped regions will be revealed over time.

I remember walking for two hours in Italy trying to find somewhere delicious for breakfast and in hungry desperation settling for a floppy toastie with other crabby tourists. Just up the road and round the corner sat the most authentic little eatery packed with locals. This book is here to ensure you don't have any floppy sandwiches in Tassie.

So enjoy the journey, let the pages stir some island plans and get exploring like a local.

Alice Hansen

TAILORED TASMANIA

What the locals love

Tailored Tasmania Australia

First published in Australia in 2014 by
Alice Hansen, Hobart, Tasmania, Australia

Email: tailoredtasmania@gmail.com

National Library of Australia
Cataloguing-in-Publication data:

Author: Hansen, Alice, 1980.
Title: Tailored Tasmania.

ISBN: 978-0-9802800-5-0

1. Tailored Tasmania
I. Title. Dewey Number: A823.4
Produced in Tasmania, Australia

Design: Lea Crosswell

Editing: Impress: clear communication

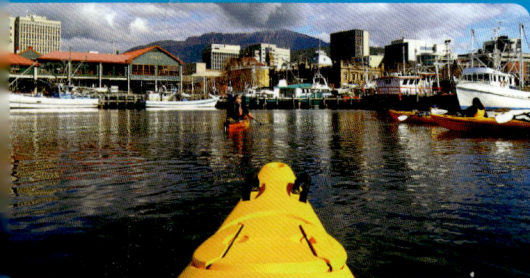

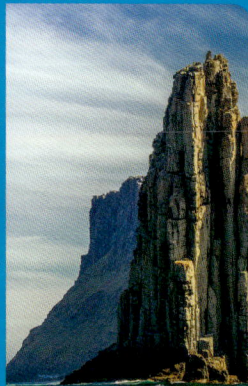

Hobart City

KELLY ST

What the locals love

TIPS FROM THOSE WHO LIVE HERE

Inner City — including Salamanca, Battery Point, North Hobart and more

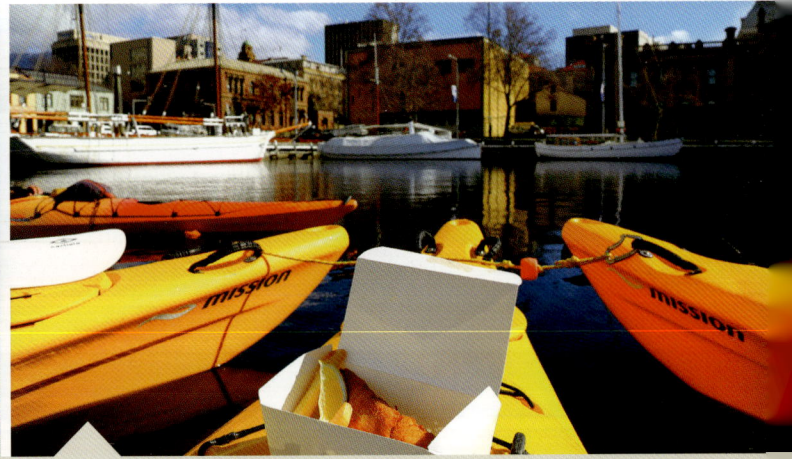

> It's not an everyday combination — but it should be. Japanese tapas and jazz tunes are on the menu every Friday at Jam Jar in Battery Point. Check the blackboard behind the counter, and if there's still room among the locals, pop your name on the list!

> There's a reason colonial artist John Glover painted up at Knocklofty Reserve. Follow in his footsteps across bushland used by early settlers for firewood and grazing. Sitting snugly behind the suburb of West Hobart, the city views are pretty and trails will lead you past quarries and other pieces of the past.

> Explore the River Derwent from the seat of a kayak. This is particularly special during the Wooden Boat Festival, and on the local tour you'll be served fresh fish and chips from the nearby fish punt, direct to your kayak's deck!

> Some say the outlook from Mount Nelson trumps a trip up Mount Wellington. Sweeping views of the Channel certainly feel closer from this vantage point and the café's freshly baked scones rival the setting. It's also beautiful at night.

> Up for a night at the theatre? Slip into a comfy red velvet chair at the Theatre Royal, Australia's oldest continuously-operating theatre.

> Those who love a good farmers market can't go past the Farm Gate Market (every Sunday) in Hobart or the Bream Creek Market (held monthly) for the freshest produce we have to offer.

> Sit down by the water's edge at Cornelian Bay – grab a coffee and pick your favourite boatshed from the shoreline.

> Dinner in North Hobart and an arty movie at the State is a popular combination. From a casual bite at the Winston to tapas at Raincheck or the new wine bar next door, this strip is the local's haven for eating out.

> Nestled away in Lenah Valley you'll find Lady Franklin Gallery, open to the public on weekends. The stone gallery was built in 1842 as a museum dedicated to art and history, created by Lady Jane Franklin to encourage "cultural aspirations".

> Everyone loves a lazy few hours in a bean bag, especially if it's pink and on the lawns outside Australia's largest private art collection. There's nothing like some Tassie sparkling in the sunshine at MONA. Catch a concert on the lawns or enjoy the market during summer.

> Anyone for bus bingo in a former Metro bus at Preachers? The hand-pumped Two Metre Tall ale is the ideal match.

> "My friends and I are riding our bikes from the city out to MONA on the weekend as the weather looks nice. The bike track they have now allows you to do that safely – especially because we will have to rehydrate with a Moo Brew once we're out there."

> "We love strolling along Sandy Bay's Long Beach and a picnic on the grass with pizza from Sandy Bay Woodfired Pizza ... yum!"

> Wander around the market at the Masonic temple on a Sunday to discover a host of local makers, then sit and enjoy St Davids Park over the road, the city's first cemetery.

> Hop on the swings at Arthurs Circus in Battery Point, surrounded by quaint 1800s cottages.

> Climb the steps of Nanny Goat Lane in Battery Point, with views out to the mountain.

HOBART CITY

> Keep an eye out for old-fashioned security measures – old sandstone walls with broken glass embedded across the top. A laneway off Collins Street, which in the 1870s separated a Catholic girls' orphanage and the boys' school of Hutchins, is a fine example. There are similar walls dotted around Salamanca Square.

> Who doesn't like free live music? Rektango comes to life every Friday evening in the Salamanca Arts Centre courtyard from 5.30pm. Run by the musicians themselves, and with a quarry wall as their backdrop, it doesn't get more relaxed than a gypsy jig and a local brew with this crowd.

> At Marieville Esplanade watch the neighbourhood dogs bound happily.

> Grab a D'Angelos pizza and head for Princes Park for an evening eating in the outdoors.

> Brunch at Ginger Brown or Picnic Basket down Taroona way – great for friends with dogs. Miss Watson is a menu favourite.

> Take the Hobart Rivulet track from the city. It'll lead you up to Cascade Brewery – now that's a destination worth walking for. It's Australia's oldest brewery – we set up the important things first ...

HOBART CITY

> Like the idea of live music onboard a former Sydney to Hobart yacht on the River Derwent? Give Hobart Yachts a call and they can arrange anything from a venture to the Jurassic-like south-west of Tasmania, to a champagne breakfast off the coast of Bruny Island.

> Looking for a peaceful area to enjoy a summer barbecue? Just five minutes from the city, Waterworks Reserve is a favourite for family birthdays and runners looking for challenging trails (yes, we did slide down the dam wall on our tummy during a boot camp session but we don't advise you to do the same). Take a walk from the Waterworks up to Fern Tree for a completely different view of Hobart. You can enjoy a long Sunday lunch at the Fern Tree Tavern then wander your way back down the hill.

What the locals love

Christie Sweeting's LOCAL TIPS

Hobart is made for winter. It' the perfect time of year to mooch around and if it gets too cold head for a café or bar. Then there are the festivals: Dark Mofo, Festival of Voices ...

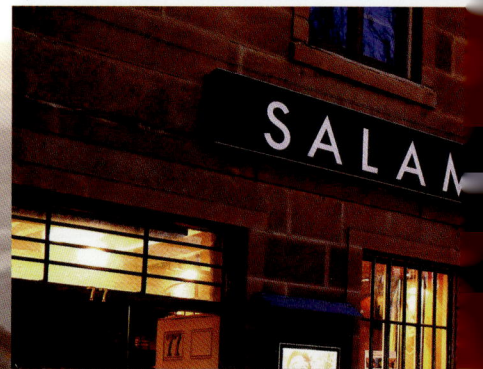

The Mountain – she looks different every day. You could spend a lifetime up there and never stop discovering things. Great tracks include the Icehouse Track – from the top the view takes in Bruny, the south-west and Tasman Peninsula. Wandering on the lower slopes is fun. You come across moss-covered huts which were razed in the '67 fires; the only bits to survive are old tools, stone walls and the chimney.

Hinsby Beach in Taroona is popular in the summertime with locals looking for a dip

Fossicking: I love discovering lovely pre-loved objects, furniture and clothing in antique shops. Favourites are the shop on Warwick Street, North Hobart, and the shop on Macquarie Street, South Hobart.

For the Arts: The Salamanca Arts Centre precinct – Spacebar Gallery has loads of beautiful things, most of which are produced in Tasmania. All things MONA, of course.

Treats: LUC. in South Hobart. I want to move in. Store & Co always has a treasure trove of things. Beautiful fashion, vintage finds and furniture.

Eats and drinks: So many choices! Smolt – breakfast, lunch, dinner and everything in between. Bottega Rotolo – cheese heaven. Loads of delicious treats – but I can't get past the cheese. I suggest having a coffee or glass of wine while you contemplate what cheese to buy. Eaglehawk Inn – fabulous bottle shop. New Sydney – fab pub with delicious cider on tap. Preachers – ever evolving and in winter I suggest you try their warm cider with a good measure of spiced Sailor Jerry rum for that extra warmth.

The river: being on the water and looking back at beautiful Hobart takes my breath away.

Entertainment: State Cinema in any season. Perfect on a rainy Sunday afternoon – try and get cinema five in the cellars. Leather sofas, fluffy foot rug with a glass of wine. Theatre Royal – what a venue – it has a fantastic program every year. And of course the Tasmanian Symphony Orchestra (TSO).

Why I love my house: 30 minutes walk from the city but the house is a sanctuary for native wildlife. We have a wallaby living in the front garden, a family of bandicoots in the back garden and a very sweet ringtail possum in the roof. ●

HOBART CITY

15

A Weekend with Liza-Jane

Meet North Hobart's Liza-Jane. This bubbly local loves entertaining visitors and whisking them away to her favourite spots. Whether you live here or plan to visit, this is a weekend you're going to want to borrow!

Friday night we'd head to Grape for bubbles and tapas then round to Rektango for some live music. Saturday would start with perhaps a yoga session at IXL Lounge down at Hunter Street followed by breakkie at an artisan bakery such as Daci & Daci or Pigeon Hole. Then it'd be off to Salamanca Market and shopping nearby – Spacebar Gallery, The Maker, Rebecca Roth and Handmark Gallery are my favourites, then we'd hit the Hobart Bookshop.

Next, we'd stroll back up to NoHo (aka North Hobart) pop into Tusk for some more retail therapy before catching a flick at the State Cinema – checking out the bookstore there too. After, we'd treat ourselves to an old-fashioned milkshake and lollies at Renown before heading to either Raincheck, Berta, Smolt or Ethos for dinner.

Sunday, we'd hit the Farmers Market for an organic egg and bacon roll and a great coffee. We'd then stock up on some of Masaaki's sushi before hiring bikes to ride out to MONA. We'd eat our sushi on the pink bean bags and wash it down with some Muse bubbles. We'd spend the afternoon at MONA – with more bubbles at the Void Bar in the museum to top off the day.

Alternately, another great weekend would be spent on Bruny Island. We would hit the road after collecting fresh produce and head down the Channel, stocking up on more gourmet produce along the way – Get Shucked Oysters, Bruny Island Cheese and bread, and treats from the smokehouse. I might even consider overnighting on the island as there are some great new accommodation places. Or, as the ultimate weekend escape I'd rent our very own island in the D'Entrecasteaux Channel – Satellite Island. Really, look that place up, it's incredible! ●

Liza Jane Sowden

Tips from Cam Tapp on how to enjoy a Tassie weekend

Ever wondered what Cam Tapp (from The Voice) likes to do when he returns to his much-loved birthplace of Tasmania? Follow the tracks of this famous singer-songwriter next time you're here, as Cam describes what he and a mate might get up to on a weekend in Tassie.

HOBART CITY

If a friend and I were in Tassie for the weekend, I'd have to of course start by having drinks at Knoppies (Knopwood's Retreat in Salamanca) on the Friday night and then maybe a fisherman's basket at Mures for dinner followed by a stroll through Salamanca later that night.

On Saturday we'd wander down through Battery Point to Salamanca Market for a coffee at Retro Café. If it was a nice day then maybe a drive up to the mountain and after that an arvo drive for a counter meal and a cold beer in a country pub down the Huon.

On Saturday night I'd go see a movie at the State Cinema and then grab a late meal in North Hobart. Sunday would be for going walking on one of the beautiful beaches that are within 20 minutes drive of the city. ●

Take a look at www.famoustasmanians.com.au, a brilliant website that sees Cam travel around his homeland and gain inspiration from the people and places that make this island so special.

LUC.

LUC. is a design store established by Lucy Given. Lucy was involved in the interior design and architecture industry for over 20 years and has now curated and collected an amazing range of homewares, design product and fashion in her first solo retail business.

Lucy returned to Hobart just over five years ago having first moved away in the 80s. Living in Sydney, Melbourne and London, then Brisbane and Byron Bay (with many returns to Hobart in between). She was determined to put all her knowledge of products and design into a much-dreamed-about retail outlet and bring quality, exciting, unique retail to a town previously shy on international product.

"I like to choose products that are not only beautiful to look at but serve well as a piece of design. Form and function. I like to think I present these in a sophisticated way at LUC. I love the simple lines of Scandinavian product and I search for well-made products that can become a beautiful addition in your home, or a piece of clothing that you will wear often, because the pieces are not ruled by trend but by a classic aesthetic.

"Having lived away for quite a while it didn't make sense to me that I kept heading interstate or overseas to buy beautiful, unique and exciting design product. Hobart consumers are well educated and appreciate good design. Tasmania produces some brilliant design and there are great stores selling local designers' products, but I still felt there was a gap in the market for introducing well-recognised quality international pieces.

"I spent my entire schooling life in Hobart and in my 20s I held the belief that success, and 'life' in general, was only going to be available in another city, state or country.

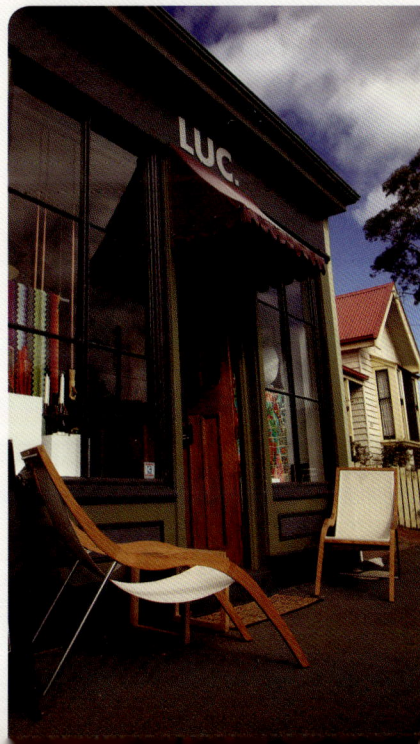

"But I love what has happened to Hobart in the last few years – I returned to the state just as MONA was starting construction and now on the wave of this extraordinary venture there is a genuine feeling of optimism, pride and excitement about what Tasmania has to offer. The food, the restaurants, the wine, the art, the music and now there's some great retail also coming through. Whenever I travel I seek out great experiences – whether that be the food and wine, entertainment or the shopping and I know that is what travellers expect when they come to Hobart – but the local population is discerning and demanding of that too and rightly so! There is a saying 'a rising tide lifts all boats' and this is exactly what we are beginning to experience in Hobart – and I am so excited to be a small part of it!" ●

Metal Urges – Chris Hood

Hidden away up a staircase in Hobart's CBD is a very passionate young Master Jeweller. His name is Chris Hood and he's travelled from Madagascar to Burma to the secret streams of Tasmania's north-east in search of gems that happy couples slip on one another's fingers to mark a lifetime commitment. We met with Chris to find out more about this dedicated Hobartian.

It all began tinkering away in his father's workshop as a young boy. His father's range of power and traditional tools kept Chris busily crafting away – skills he later refined while attending The Hutchins School in southern Tasmania. But little did his wine-making family (Hood Wines) know that these early skills would eventually take Chris across the world and often deep underground seeking out high quality diamonds and rare gems.

Today Chris heads up Tasmania's largest team of qualified jewellers and designers. Plus, when local folk (or those across the world in fact) order a diamond, platinum or 18ct gold engagement ring, they speak and work directly with the jeweller who handcrafts their piece. When I was visiting, the professional, cheerful team

were handing out handmade caramel slice, but it's the work they create when their heads are down that shines a spotlight on this boutique business.

Spend some time with Chris, and you'll understand why every piece is a one-off, beautifully-crafted work of art. What's more, we rarely think of the effort involved in the creation. Three to four times a year Chris ventures off overseas, his passport stamped in some of the most remote corners of the planet, to bring high-quality gems back to his home island.

"Gems are predominantly a visual event. You cannot buy gems from a photo, you need to see and handle them," explains Chris. "A stone has to communicate with you – you need to fall in love with it. All our gems have that extra something special."

For Chris, many of his closest friends are in the trade. "I'll get a sneaky heads-up from someone who is thinking of going to a far-flung gem mine, say in Sri Lanka or Madagascar. We won't know what we're going to find when we get there but next thing you know you're on a plane. It's exciting."

Chris talks of the amazing things that have happened; when multi-million dollar stones have been discovered in front of him. As an early riser, he loves to move around a mining settlement as day breaks. That's when he realises he's in a place where few if any other jewellery designers have ever stood, a place that his business allows him to stand.

But it doesn't all happen at the mine site. "You might get a tug on your sleeve while crossing a guest house car park in Sri Lanka followed by, 'sir, my father has a stone he'd like to show you' and you wind up in a local village with a rice farmer who found a stone in one of his waterways. Most people who live in those areas have small collections of stones. If you can connect with them sometimes that can be very special."

Naturally, Chris winds up going to his fair share of weddings. So what's the moment that really moves him? "Watching the wedding rings going on and the words that get said. I'm a mess by then," admits Chris. And he loves the idea that a hundred years on, someone might turn over the ring, see the Metal Urges logo and know the piece was well made, still wearable and doing well. It's a legacy that everyone in the business holds close.

"It's not uncommon for an interstate couple to come to Tassie for a lovely weekend away. They've heard about MONA, they like good food and a proposal is made. They come to us and see a stone they never even considered existed, at the very place they got engaged, perhaps a sapphire I've found in a wild Tasmanian river. It then fits perfectly with their story – a beautiful setting, a personally-crafted ring – they just love it."

So why does Chris choose Hobart as home? He travels two months of the year through interesting and challenging places, some of which are very beautiful. But he can't beat Tassie. Here, it takes him 10 minutes to get to work, and that's on foot. Here, the rivers are close for him to go fishing. Here, he can enjoy some of the best abalone and oysters on the planet.

"Living on an island our ethos is much like many small businesses here, where our focus is on high quality, not mass production. Tasmania forces this in a way; the whole place is about individual, unique experiences. Locals don't want generic, they want personal, so that's what we deliver."

When he's not brewing his own beer, Chris enjoys a good ale at the West End Pumphouse and is rather partial to a coffee from Villino, round the corner from Metal Urges. Where to next? Chris doesn't know himself, but one thing he does know is that Tasmania will always be home. ●

metalurges.com.au

HOBART CITY

Oyster & Pearl

You know that feeling when you stumble across a hidden treasure? When you walk up a non-descript staircase off a main street and wonder what's at the top? Well, Lou Whiting has one special treat for people who delight in the unexpected.

There before me is a studio dressed in nautical style and brimming with handmade one-off pieces. And when I say nautical I don't mean sailor hats and tacky sails, but an eclectic collection of ship-shape props that seemingly blend as tastefully as Lou's limited edition range.

When you meet Lou, she'll throw her arms in the air with humble abandon. "Sometimes I like to say the maker isn't in today," she says with a laugh. But behind that dismissive manner is a very talented lady. Lou loves fine textiles and her functional design can be felt as I eye every piece. This lady knows style. She thrives on travelling far and bringing exquisite fabrics back to her seaside home.

"Sometimes I like to say the maker isn't in today."

Once home, Lou sets about sketching, refining then sewing in small runs. There are one-off pieces in cotton, linen, silk and wool, depending which way the wind blows. One only needs to spend a few minutes in Lou's company to realise this creative spirit is without doubt "the maker" at Oyster & Pearl. Her enthusiasm is contagious and her eye for detail, so precise.

With Lou, whatever she wears, it looks good. Whatever she throws together on a shelf looks gorgeously right. Lou could make an apple look fantastic beside a stuffed wombat. Crafting designs for women of every age — her garments are made for those who appreciate feeling good in a special hand-made piece. And when she's not busily drafting new designs she enjoys a mojito by the fire at Jack Greene. ●

**Find Lou on Level 1,
147 Elizabeth Street, Hobart**
oysterandpearl.com.au
facebook.com/oysterandpearlhobart

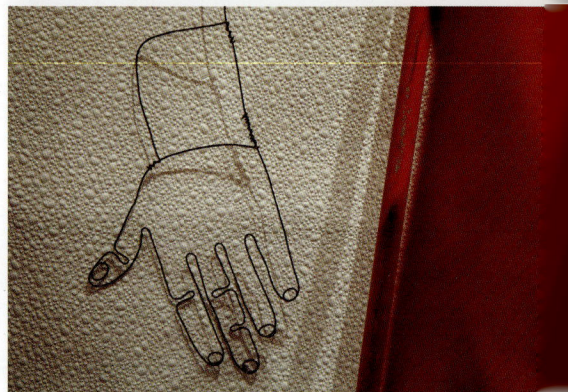

"I love to relax at the end of a long day with my wife Lyn, a dram of good whisky and a little chocolate."

Lark Distillery – *Tasmania's oldest distillery*

Lark Distillery was the first licensed distillery in Tasmania since 1839. It was established to produce Tasmanian malt whisky, rich in character with a big finish using the finest Tasmanian ingredients. Lark Distillery is very proudly a boutique distillery dedicated to maintaining its proven high-quality malt whisky and other unique Tasmanian spirits.

An exceptional single malt

Lark whisky is proudly unique in character and style, crafted in small batches exclusively from pure Tasmanian ingredients. All Lark whisky is matured in small barrels, hand-bottled by whisky lovers in Tasmania for whisky lovers worldwide.

Welcome to the whisky bar and cellar door

Situated on the Hobart waterfront, Lark whisky bar offers visitors the opportunity to taste Tasmania's finest whisky and other distilled spirits in a warm and inviting atmosphere. From great coffees and snacks to live country roots and bluegrass bands every Friday and Saturday night, this eclectic bar is a mecca for both locals and visitors alike!

Come and visit the distillery

Lark offers a variety of tours to suit your time availability. From a guided tasting at the Lark Whisky Bar to a full day of immersion in the art and craft of single malt production, visitors can chose the tour that best suits their needs.

Half-day whisky tour
Weekdays: 9.00am and 1.30pm

Tour guests travel to the distillery complex in the Coal River Valley to spend over two hours of absorbing interpretation and tasting in the pristine surroundings of the vineyards and farms in Tasmania's premium cold climate wine region. The tour concludes back at the bar where guests continue tasting and have the opportunity to purchase Lark products at special discount rates.

Full-day whisky tour
Weekdays: 8.15am to 4.30pm

Visitors spend the morning at the distillery in the Coal River Valley, followed by a visit to historic Richmond for morning tea. Lunch is at the Frogmore Creek visitors centre and includes tastings and a tour of the Tom Samek floor installation. The afternoon is spent at the distillery to see Copper Pot Stills in full operation and the barrel bond store before we return to the cellar door for guided tastings. The tour includes lunch, morning and afternoon teas, tastings and transport. ●

Lark Whisky Bar and Cellar Door
14 Davey Street, Hobart
Phone (03) 6231 9088
larkdistillery.com.au

Founder Bill Lark says their success stems from starting small and thinking big. *"Like many of Tasmania's other premium food and beverage businesses, our success stems from small-scale production of high-quality, high-value products,"* Bill said.

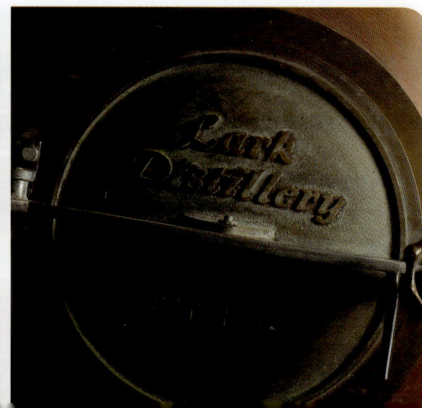

"I thought people might think we were trying to teach the Scots how to suck eggs and they would think – what are you doing you silly colonial? We make whisky, you make beer! But in fact it's been exactly the opposite. We have had tremendous support from the single malt industry worldwide, and from consumers. They were always a little nervous at the start ... but it really didn't take long for the market to truly grab hold of the fact that Tasmania can produce stunning single malt whisky."

The vision of producing Tasmanian malt whisky was born on a trout fishing trip in the highlands of Tasmania. Bill's father-in-law Max produced a wonderful bottle of single malt, and as they enjoyed a drink in the park at Bothwell, surrounded by Georgian buildings, barley fields and the gentle flowing of the Clyde River, Bill remarked to Max, *"I wonder why there isn't anyone making malt whisky in Tasmania".*

Montacute Boutique Bunkhouse

If you're parting with $40 for a night's accommodation, would you demand a garden brimming with plums, figs, elderberries and sage for your cooking pleasure, soft Tasmanian wool blankets, a shiny red bike to cruise the town, an open fire for cocktail hour and an invitation to stroll with the owner and his cute bulldog of an evening? Perhaps not. But at Montacute Boutique Bunkhouse, owners Rose and Antony have thought through every fine detail to be sure it's more than just a place to rest your head.

Rose and winemaker Ant, together with Eve (9), Lily the miniature Australian bulldog and "Mrs" the tortoiseshell cat form the welcome team at this stylishly restored 1895 Battery Point mansion. It is unlikely Captain William Langdon, the great-great-great-great-great grandfather of Ant, who left Montacute in Somerset back in 1821 bound for Tasmania, could have imagined an elegant bunkhouse would bare the name of his much-loved home village.

Some 193 years on, what can a group of girlfriends coming for a long overdue weekend away in Hobart expect during a stay at Montacute?

They might book a four-bed bunkroom, staying in on the first night to enjoy wine and cheese by the open fire, cooking for themselves and eating at the original German Oktoberfest dining table. During summer they might mix themselves a round of gin and tonics, then grab a picnic rug for the garden or head to the upper cocktail balcony, to while away the evening enjoying the panoramic view of Mount Wellington.

Crisp cotton linen and chatter into the night might be followed by an early morning bike ride across the Tasman Bridge to Bellerive Quay, catching the water taxi (with trusty bikes) back at 10am for a wander through Salamanca Market. A short walk to the waterfront and the girls can depart via high-speed ferry for MONA before wandering back to Montacute to pretty themselves for an evening out.

A five-minute walk down historic Kelly's Steps will lead them to the bars, artist studios, live music and restaurants of Salamanca. Or they may just stroll around the corner to Monty's on Montpelier to be treated by Terry and his talented team to a six-course degustation with matched wines. Now what's on for tomorrow? A Pennicott Wilderness Journeys eco-adventure cruise alongside frolicking seals, whales and dolphins perhaps? ●

Montacute at a glance

- Private double rooms with queen bed
- Private, mixed and girls-only bunkrooms
- Schwinn Cream 7-speed bikes $5/hour or $25/day
- Free wifi throughout
- Spacious, well-equipped kitchen
- Extensive herb and vegetable garden
- Free off-street parking

montacute.com.au

HOBART CITY

Gourmania – *let a sixth-generation local take you on a tasting journey*

Throw on some comfy shoes and grab your appetite – that's all you'll need for your Gourmania food tour, as your locally-grown guide takes you on a food-fuelled gourmet journey through Hobart's inner city.

Today we partake in the City Tour, one of four unique tour options. This tour begins in the historic Salamanca area and will return here at the end of the four-hour experience.

There's nothing like salmon for breakfast and to start our morning we taste delicious cured and smoked Tasmanian Atlantic Salmon. We pick up some interesting facts along the way, about Tasmania's lucrative seafood industry and about the transformation of the Salamanca strip into the foodie hub it is today. After checking out the café that started it all in 1990, we move on to a little taste of heaven at a local deli – home to Wagyu smoked brisket, house-made terrines and much much more!

A short stroll through a former cemetery, now a verdant park, and we have made our way into the city. Here at a legendary local patisserie we take a break for coffee and are lured into eating flaky pastries made with (at least) 50% butter. Worth every tasty morsel!

Moving on through the main shopping area of downtown, home to the prettiest dresses and most stylish homewards, we enjoy super fresh sushi maki. Before you know it it's 11 o'clock and time for wine! We are told, and we are happy to believe it, that the palate is most receptive to discerning the subtleties of wine before lunch time. We indulge in a tasting guided by an industry professional with over 25 years experience. The range on the bench are mostly local drops from small producers – delicious wines, many of which never make it off the island.

Next, at Australia's second-oldest continuously-licensed pub we enjoy an impressive dish of fresh calamari, complete with parsnip chips, then on to a wonderfully-aromatic spice shop where you can pick up native pepper berries or locally-grown saffron. A still-warm-from-the-oven cinnamon pastry has us in raptures as we make our way back to the

waterfront to enjoy our next generous taste. Stunning views of the docks are ours as we bite into juicy, fresh, cooked fish – they serve whatever is freshest that day.

Returning to the Salamanca area we visit a cheesemonger's, where we try a handful of cheeses as well as lush spiced cherries and local raw honeys. Our final stop is a stylish restaurant where we choose a scoop of house-made ice-cream or sorbet – a sweet touch at the end of this incredibly varied and comprehensive overview of the city and its amazing food. Our eyes have been opened to this foodie paradise, where the best produce is only an arm's reach away. ●

Call 0419 180 113 for bookings or visit gourmaniafoodtours.com.au

Sanctum – *treat yourself in Sandy Bay*

We had a little chat with the owner of Sanctum, Dr Asha McCartney, about what inspires her.

Tell us about yourself and how you came to call Hobart home.

I am a traveller! Born in Fiji with an idyllic island childhood, I won a scholarship to study Medicine in Australia. I was drawn subconsciously to an island again, choosing Tasmania for my studies despite the obvious weather differences. Over the next 20 years, my studies, work and adventures have taken me to Canada, the UK, Europe, Asia, Africa and South America. Inevitably, the pull of island life was too great and we settled back in Hobart to establish a family and professional life.

What is the inspiration behind Sanctum and what do you hope to create within its walls?

Sanctum was born out of necessity and evolved very rapidly over a period of six months. Quite simply, I tried to create an ultimate urban skin sanctuary, one that I wished existed. Sanctum simply unfolded like a flower blooming – with spontaneous un-choreographed progression.

Tell us about your love of art, interior design and how this fits into the Sanctum story.

I realise I have always been a very visually-stimulated person. As well as pursuing a career essentially in the sciences, I come from a very artistic family, and have always had a parallel interest in the visual arts, design, fashion, travel and music. It was inevitable that all these interests crept into the Sanctum concept. Sanctum is a destination ... an experience and a professional space all in one.

In your eyes, what makes Sanctum special?

Sanctum makes you feel different once you have entered the space. All your senses are stimulated and that evokes an immediate emotional response. You feel nurtured, valued and restored. In our frenetic, technology-based lives, this personal "rebooting" is incredibly restorative and is not only desirable, but I would argue is vital for each of us functioning at our full potential and living our best lives. I feel so fortunate to love my job! It is the perfect blend of science and art and people and technology. It remains a daily privilege to share in people's lives and I value the trust my patients place in me. Their response to my services drives me to excellence.

Latest venture?

This year I'm visiting and working in three international clinics – in New York and Boston in the US and I have just finished working with the internationally-renowned plastic surgeon Dr Herve Raspaldo in Cannes, France, on a one-on-one basis. The intense collaboration means I can continue to bring the best of international knowledge, technology and techniques to Hobart. My mantra is that people value excellence whether they live in NY, the French Riviera or Hobart.

What do you love about Hobart?

The incredible freshness of every day. Cleanest air, bluest skies, the ability in a 10-minute drive to work to see the ever-changing River Derwent, two beaches and Mt Wellington. I feel so lucky to live here.

Favourite coffee spot?

Hobart is full of fantastic coffee spots! We are big fans of Pilgrim Coffee in Argyle Street. Will and his team have created a vibrant urban space with some of the most innovative food and most consistent coffee around!

Will you share a local secret with us?

The breakfast bruschetta at Zum Café in Salamanca. I've been ordering this for years and friends still get food envy when they see it arrive at the table ... a deadly-delicious taste sensation combining goats cheese, basil pesto, Tasmanian mushrooms and a drizzle of balsamic glaze.

What's your favourite day out?

Without question a day out on the water on the River Derwent on our yacht Serengeti, my iPhone with my new music finds of the week, the papers, a picnic lunch and some chilled rosé! ●

72 Sandy Bay Road, Sandy Bay
sanctummedical.com.au

Raincheck Lounge

When I sat down to have a chat to Carl at Raincheck to learn about what makes this place hum, I could barely hear him. The gaggle of locals was such that I had to lean in with a smile and do my best to talk over the masses. It was 9.20am on a random weekday. But as is the way with Raincheck, the tables were already full to the brim and coffees were briskly being delivered around me.

Carl, who has been at it for 10 years and about to open a wine bar next door with some mates, just smiles back at me in between giving directions to a builder for some kitchen work. It's busy, and the atmosphere is happy and lively. No wonder people love coming here.

The little café/bar/restaurant has been a favourite long before the North Hobart strip became a bustling foodies' haven. Open for breakfast, lunch and dinner every day of the week you can push open their door at practically any time and see something on the menu that suits. Specialising in tapas, Raincheck is also the place to share with good friends and good wine.

It was news to me that the word tapas means "cover" and refers to the covering of bread that bartenders in Spain used to place on top of drinks to keep the dust and flies away. Over time, the word has evolved to a term given to bar snacks that Raincheck do rather well.

In a relaxed social style, Raincheck has re-invented some classic tapas and also has a chef's table on the blackboard that changes, from which you can order four shared courses with bread and salad to share for a set price. It

really doesn't matter if you're after a quick snack or a long dinner after a State Cinema movie across the way.

For a fairly snug venue, Raincheck has an impressive menu. Whether you're after minted pea and goats cheese arancini, lamb kofta with tzatziki and flat bread or east coast vongole in a chorizo and beer broth, they have you covered. And for breakfast, the spinach and Heidi gruyere omelette with toast is a treat.

Before I'd closed my notebook, Carl bid a friendly farewell and was off to help out in the kitchen. The Raincheck show must go on — and I wished him well on the wine bar next door, which will undoubtedly allow the Raincheck love to spread further along the North Hobart strip. ●

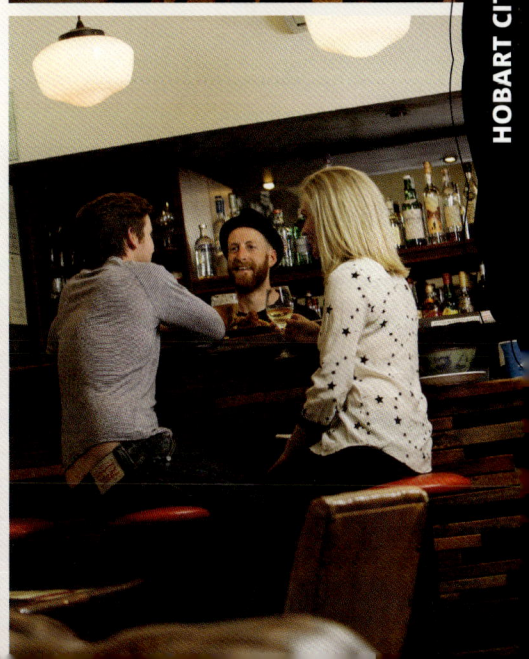

HOBART CITY

Zimmah Coffee

"I got into coffee accidentally – three months shy of a computer science degree," explains Dane Knezevic, sitting in the comfy fit-out of his Murray Street Zimmah Café. "I'd always said I'd take a different career to my father's but when he fell sick I was needed at Island Espresso."

The family had spent their lives in hospitality, Dane's father buying Island for his wife, a place she and her two daughters used to frequent as customers. When cancer struck, it was Dane who stepped into his father's role and some 10 years on is loving the industry he promised his father he'd avoid.

When two of his friends encouraged him to join forces in 2011 the Zimmah brand was born. In the beginning, it was bare-bones roasting. No retail. No fancy branding. Just roasting incredibly good coffee. Before Dane knew it though, Zimmah began to take on a personality of its own. Soon wholesale buyers were settling in for coffees in Murray Street and suggesting a café should open. And their single origin and blended coffees were badged with names and characters never seen in the coffee industry. There were no beans or coffee cups on the Zimmah packaging – there were bushrangers and tattooed nuns.

Not long after the left-of-centre branding took hold, Zimmah were serving 400 coffees an hour at The Taste Festival and people were falling in love with the "shonky barman" and asking for "devil and the deep" by name, each based on a Tasmanian story.

For a boy who left Tasmania at 16 to pursue a soccer career, chosen for the Australian schoolboys side only to return to Hobart because he missed the place, the Zimmah story is a special one. "I missed my mum and my sisters during those two years away. I just had to come home."

Today, just as always, Dane loves being part of the Hobart community. He's forged strong friendships and will often wander down to Salamanca Market to chat with the boys who serve up his coffee to the locals and visitors.

So what makes a good coffee? While I braced for a complex response involving particle size, grinding techniques, tampering and temperature, I got three letters. TLC. According to Dane, it's all about the love and care afforded to each cup. Of course, there's a whole science that goes behind what makes a coffee good – but for Dane attention to detail is paramount.

You only have to hop on the Zimmah website to understand the level of passion that Dane possesses: "Coffee roasting is an art just as historic and elaborate as any other: a mixture of intuition and manual hand response."

And when Dane is not roasting or overseeing the daily workings at Zimmah, where does he like to dine? "Garagiste – it doesn't matter whether you go with someone or by yourself. I just enjoy sitting at the bar. They're so attentive and there's been plenty of times that I've been joined by someone who is there alone, simply to enjoy the dining experience. And it's not just because they serve Zimmah coffee – their food is brilliant!" ●

zimmah.com.au

Dutch Courage

Dutch Courage draws inspiration from a time when bootleggers and makeshift distilleries ran rampant in the colonies. If you like your coffee with just a little bit of bite, the sweet, fruity flavours and liqueur-like texture are exactly what the doctor ordered.

Characteristics: Aniseed, pecan nuts, cooking chocolate, molasses, dark berries, unripe strawberries, sugar cane.

Tattooed Nun

Tattooed Nun is all about contrast and balance. On one hand, as a black it offers the ultimate guilty pleasure – rich with buttery caramel flavours and a dark chocolate finish. On the other hand, add milk to the mix and you will be presented with a much more controlled and smooth experience. The only question is which one will you choose?

Characteristics: Molasses, dried raisin, stone fruits, dark chocolate, creamy mouth feel, mild acidity, pecan, vanilla, heavy body, juicy.

eat

HOBART CITY

Elliott My Dear

Ever wondered what it's like to be an artist in Hobart? Elliott My Dear creates prints and accessories from Sarah Elliot's oil paintings using the highest-quality inks, archival paper and recycled paper. Sarah has a Bachelor of Fine Arts from Melbourne University and works full time as an artist. Elliott My Dear has a stall at Hobart's Salamanca Market and supplies to shops all over the country. Sarah exhibits work locally and interstate and is in private collections throughout Australia.

Tell us about Elliot My Dear and how it came to be.

I started painting again after a big break and just wanted to do something that was true to myself. I was really surprised when other people understood my work and where I was coming from. I was even more pleased when people appreciated the sentiment and feeling that goes into each painting – I haven't stopped painting since!

What do you love most about being an artist here in Hobart?

I love the lifestyle you can have in Hobart and the huge support there is for local artists. I also love what an attractive and friendly city Hobart is. There is always something beautiful to paint here!

How does Tasmania shape your creative work?

A distant horizon and a sense of being on an island is always part of my work. I love colonial architecture with its often raw and exposed state. Being from England I think a lot about what it means to be here, our impact, and the positive contribution we can make.

The evocative and sweet characters in your prints – what inspires these?

The people in my paintings are characters that are part of a narrative. They express the feelings of events and speak of the things that are hard to put into words – themes of love, family, loss and hope. My characters are always inspired by a psychological space that evolves as I paint; I find it is only revealed to me at the end and I go, "ahh, that's what it's about". I tend to work very intuitively.

Favourite coffee spot?

Capulus Espresso North Hobart. I love sitting on a milk crate in the sun before heading in to my studio. But for a long chat with a friend I always go to Fullers, I love being surrounded by all the books and their inspiration.

Will you share a local secret with us?

If you walk along the South Hobart rivulet, towards the women's prison, there's a tall sharp cliff with large convict bricks cut into it – but they weren't taken out, they must have stopped half way. I run my fingers along all the nicks and close my eyes – it's like going back in time.

What's your favourite day out?

My family and I love playing in the snow on Mt Wellington. It's like another world up there. I love the sense of wonder, the changing light, the big boulders and tiny trees. The city looks like it's in miniature with little hills and seas that go on forever. ●

elliottmydear.blogspot.com.au

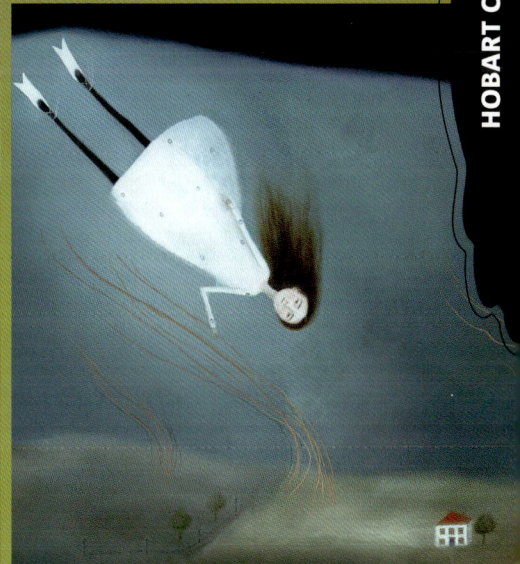

Rebecca Roth Gallery

Rebecca Roth is a resin jewellery and homewares designer based in Hobart. Her pocket space gallery is located in the Salamanca Arts Centre alcove and is often likened to a lolly shop, with its brightly-coloured handmade pieces lining the windows. Always redefining herself, Rebecca recently began hand pouring small batches of lightly scented soy candles. Wander by and you'll likely meet the maker at work, or of a Saturday at her Salamanca Market stall. We met with Rebecca to find out more about being a Hobart designer.

Where did it all begin?

In 2004, I began threading gemstones, pearl necklaces and kilt pins (I hear you say what? Kilt pins?) Yep I did, for my friends' birthdays and weddings. I have always loved resin jewellery, its colours and texture, and have had a fascination with designing. I bought my first resin supplies in 2006 and began playing. It took some time over the next year to become familiar with the medium and to learn, trust and master the process of mixing, pouring and polishing my early pieces.

My jewellery business developed over the years and I don't recall that moment when I changed my thinking from a hobby to a business. I wish I did. It has emerged and evolved every day, and is now very much a part of my life and our family.

I began working at what I think is Australia's favourite outdoor market, Salamanca Market, in March 2006. My business grew from here. I started a website in 2007 and dreamt of starting up a creative and makers market for all of Hobart's very talented makers who I stood beside each Saturday. In early 2009 I co-founded Hobart's first art and

design market in Hobart's Masonic Hall. Later that same year I began plans of opening my small pocket space gallery in the Salamanca Arts Centre along Hobart's waterfront. These days my life has a lovely balance of family, creative play, work and rest. I wish. Actually that's my goal. I'm still working towards that!

My son was six months old when he first visited me at Salamanca market in his pram. He is now almost nine. He said to me only a few weeks ago, "Mum when I go to school do you work hard? My response was, "yes I do, very hard," thinking to myself, "well not always, mostly I go to the studio or shop to play".

At times I ponder my journey, and although there have been very busy, stressful and challenging times there have also been wonderful reflective, calm and proud moments. I love the peace in my studio, which helps me to think and create. I don't even play music.

What do I love about what I do? I love that each day is different and I love to walk along Tasmania's rugged coastlines looking for pebbles and shapes of inspiration for my work. I am always conscious of being ever so lucky to make a living out of what I LOVE to do. For that I am very grateful.

Favourite coffee spot?

The Beach House at Lower Sandy Bay, just across from a very delicious dinner venue – Sandy Bay Woodfired Pizza.

Will you share a local secret with us?

If you love to collect sea glass, head over to the waterfront around Bellerive Bluff – it's everywhere!

What's your favourite day out?

A bike ride along the pipeline track on Mt Wellington or a ferry ride over to discover Bruny Island's gems. ●

rebeccaroth.com.au

Tusk North Hobart

Partners in business, partners in crime, Jeremy Edwards and Jason Niaura having been living and working in North Hobart for over half their lives. It's in their blood. Over numerous bottles of Chardy Jeremy and Jason would constantly come up with weird and wonderful concepts. From this they developed The Concept Trust, which is where businesses including Tusk and Fusion Hairdressing (a few doors up from Tusk) have evolved. While Jason goes snippety-snip at Fusion, Jeremy can be found tangled in ribbon and wrap at Tusk.

Tell is the background of Tusk?

Tusk for us started over four years ago. I'd been working in corporate-land for a decade; at the time I worked in Hobart as Operations Manager at a training and human resources company. We lived above the salon back then and every day I would walk home past this little shop with whimsical dreams of throwing away my suits and living a fun life.

One day from work I rang Jason at the salon. I think I was having a bad day tangled in red tape. Anyway, I rang with the silly idea of buying this little shop in North Hobart and quitting my job and so on. It was more so a "what if" conversation, as we had just bought a house, so there was the mortgage etc etc. I am still not sure exactly how we took the plunge (or risk), but a month later we were signing the paperwork to buy Tusk. Six months later we had expanded the store to double the size, hired more team members, and it was taking off so well I actually quit my job for good. The Salvos were most appreciative of all of my suits!

How do you choose the eclectic mix that makes Tusk so colourful and special?

That's a hard one. We don't really have a magic formula ... I wish we did. We definitely go for eclectic and colourful. We love quirky, unusual, and tongue in cheek. We love taking risks, and I think people come to us as a result (it doesn't always work but mostly it does). We aim to keep everything at a reachable price point. We are all involved in the buying, and our customers give us heaps of feedback – so this creates the eclectic flavour of Tusk. We source the weird, wacky and wonderful from all over the globe, but also source amazing products from creative Tasmanians. It's a nice mix. Like a rainbow cake.

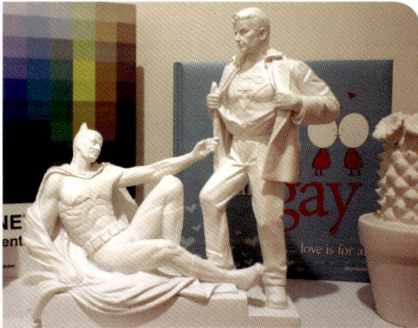

People come to you to purchase gifts for loved ones – is it satisfying when they find the perfect fit?

One fun thing about working at Tusk is the laughter you hear. We have a strong loyalty from our customer base. We always get feedback like "I've just come in for my fix". We have created an environment for the customer that's a kind of pick-me-up for a bad day. We actually have regular customers who come in during their lunch hour to play at Tusk, laugh at the cards, and so on. It's almost like a little therapy to get them through their day.

Another fun thing to watch is customers who bring in their friends to show them around. They actually love introducing their friends to Tusk as their own special place – they take a sense of pride and ownership. This is amazing to experience, and makes us feel very proud of what we are doing. I guess what we are trying to create is an experience. We want the experience and high that the buyer receives to be just as wonderful as the receiver of the gift.

What do you like about living and working in North Hobart?

The people, the atmosphere. Everyone is there for a positive reason. Food, cafés, wine bars, hotels, bookshops, beauty, hair, more food, the cinema. It's almost like the pamper strip.

Where do you like to spend your time in North Hobart?

When not playing at Tusk? I love my Saturday treat; I knock off work, wander up to the Winston, and treat myself to a pint of a different craft beer. It's friendly, relaxed, there's personalities to meet, and you get to watch the world go by.

Favourite night out with friends?

We are too spoilt for choice. I love food, and am never disappointed! A sneaky film at the State, a saunter through their bookshop, and a glass of wine is a nice weeknight treat.

Where do you go on a day out of town?

We take Olive (my niece) to Richmond. Picnic by the river, ducks to feed, a wander around the town, icecreams, fairy treasure hunting, pirate maps ... we call it adventure day! ●

The Library House

Some places don't offer your typical four-white-walled stay. Some are created to nourish and inspire. As told in the words of revered local author (and owner) Heather Rose, let's find out how Library House got its name.

By the end you'll be wanting to curl up and read a book by the open fire, or strum out a new melody with co-owner Rowan Smith. We've warned you – don't expect to step inside and not feel the creative pulse of these two passionate locals. It's not surprising that Virgin Magazine has listed Library House as one of Australia's top five new getaways.

Library House represents 17 years of love, commitment, hard work, nurture, vision and, especially, creativity. This house has been home to the writing of stories, songs and screenplays, films have been filmed here, art created. Some iconic Tasmanian brands and advertising campaigns were imagined here. Music albums have been recorded here. Novels have been written here.

It's a house that has welcomed many friends over the years. There have been countless memorable dinner parties, Christmases, birthdays, business and community celebrations, seminars and so on.

The Federation house was built in 1900, and has been owned by only four families in 114 years. Those who stay can even look over the original architect's drawing from 1900.

Why the name Library House?

From Heather: "When I was little, my favourite places to go were libraries. My dad would often take me to the State Library and I was in heaven. When I started to get pocket money, I began to buy books.

Over the years, as the books multiplied, I began to have this fantasy that one day I'd have a library to pass on. I suspected that, in time, books would become something archaic and I wanted to hand down to my great great grandchildren these beautiful relics of a completely different time. It's funny how that may yet come to pass because of e-books.

Our new home at the beach is wonderful, but it didn't have nearly enough room for our books, and so I thought, what if we left them here? What if instead of waiting for my great great grandchildren, I shared them now with whoever came to visit? That was the seed of why we created Library House – because of my library.

On the shelves there's novels from years of literary discovery, novels bought all over the world. There's a little bit of philosophy, some art, photography, poetry, all manner of non-fiction, cookbooks. There are biographies. There's everything that has organically grown through my interest in reading and writing – and even some of my childhood books. There are lots of books that have been research for my novels. And there are some special editions.

We regularly update the library with new books and classics I'm still discovering. They are all there for people to delve into, to enjoy, to discover new writers and different thoughts about the world.

The bedrooms are named after books of special significance to us. Downstairs is The Age of Innocence room, which is an Edith Wharton novel. Wharton is one of my favourite writers, but also the Martin Scorsese movie of the book was the first movie that Rowan and I went to see together. It wasn't officially a date, but I can remember beginning to fall in love with him that afternoon.

The front bedroom is called the Norwegian Wood room. It used to be Rowan's music studio. He's made a number of albums in there. Norwegian Wood is a Beatles classic and also a fabulous novel by Haruki Murakami, one of my top five favourite writers.

Upstairs the main bedroom is The River Wife room. The River Wife was my third novel, and perhaps the novel I'm most proud of, but also my least known! This room looks out on the Derwent River, which plays a significant part in the novel.

The fourth bedroom is called Light in August after William Faulkner's near-perfect novel. The fifth bedroom is called the Finding Serendipity room, after the first book in the Tuesday McGillycuddy children's series co-written with Danielle Wood. (Together we are Angelica Banks.)

Rowan likes to reassure people that despite this obsession with books, there is Foxtel for 24-hour sport and all the other channels. So whatever people's interests, there's always something to keep them entertained when they stay at Library House.

It's a home where there has been so much love and creativity, and it delights us to share that with our visitors." ●

Hobart Yachts – set sail on a former Sydney to Hobart beauty

The cries of excitement were chorusing throughout the yacht. We were on our way home after an overnight charter to the Tasman Peninsula and were greeted with the sight of up to 20 humpback whales casually swimming in the river as our passengers watched on in awe.

Hobart Yachts is the brainchild of Mark and Marsha Stranger. Their beautiful yacht, the 62-foot Helsal IV, is part of a legendary line of racing yachts that have competed in Sydney to Hobart yacht races, and sailed across the globe. Helsal IV is a racer/cruiser, meaning she is both fast and luxurious. She's based at Hobart's Kings Pier, although she spends her days exploring the Tasmanian coastline.

My first few trips on Helsal IV were as a photographer documenting the amazing places that Hobart Yachts visits. I enjoyed it so much I have since taken up a position as cook and deckhand, which has enabled me to be the ultimate male multi-tasker.

The best way to really experience the thrill of sailing on such a boat is by doing one of the overnight trips that Hobart Yachts offers. From the Tasman Peninsula and Bruny Island to the longer multi-day trips up the east coast and around the south-west wilderness to Port Davey, these charters offer a thrilling way to see Tasmania.

Our most recent trip began with an eight-hour sail in consistent 15-knot winds across Storm Bay to the Tasman Peninsula. This trip takes us past Shipstern Bluff and Cape

Raoul, whose incredible broken spires were used many years ago as target practice by the British Navy.

For much of the way, a pod of dolphins surf the wake off the bow of the boat. The freedom these animals express in the water is perhaps only matched by the graceful flight of the majestic albatross. These birds with their great wingspan are said to contain the souls of lost sailors; I could watch them all day as they ride the ocean air currents and follow us on our travels.

Once we round Cape Raoul, Tasman Island comes into view. This is the very south-east corner of Tasmania and it sits directly opposite Cape Pillar and some of the largest sea cliffs in the world.

After a day of ocean sailing and coastal exploring we head into Port Arthur, the infamous penal colony that is so embedded in Australia's European history. Port Arthur is a fantastic anchorage and a great place to sit and watch the sun go down before retiring to the warmth of the heated cabin, some good music and a home-cooked dinner.

The following day we leave for home with our dolphin escorts leading the way. The wind is up for the trip and we set a smaller jib and reef our mainsail in, so we don't have

too much sail out for the conditions. This turns out to be the perfect combination and we have the boat humming along at well over 10 knots.

As we enter Hobart's Derwent Estuary, we see plumes of spray backlit by the low afternoon sun. After years of unsustainable whaling, these elegant beasts have recently returned to the river and each year they are becoming more numerous. It is a great end to an amazing trip and highlights the fact that whether it's in our river or along our coastline, sailing in Tasmania is one of the best ways to experience this incredible place.

You'll usually find Helsal IV docked at Hobart's waterfront. ●

Words and images by Jimmy Emms

hobartyachts.com.au

HOBART CITY

you are welcome to browse

BILLIE-JO AND CALISTA

Billie-Jo and Calista are injecting life into Hobart's design scene through their creative learning hub. Since meeting in 2007 this dynamic duo have supported each other to develop their own businesses, culminating in a dream for most – a buzzing boutique boasting an in-store studio.

"The studio allows Calista to have a retail outlet for her designs and also creates interest within the store. We can offer in-store services such as tailoring and hemming of jeans; not many places can offer that," says Billie-Jo enthusiastically. "It also means I get my living room back," Calista adds.

Billie Jo, owner of the eponymous boutique, has always wanted to run her own fashion boutique. After working interstate and completing her tertiary education Billie-Jo returned to set up shop in Criterion Street and start a family. "Tasmania is the ideal place to raise my kids. My partner was convinced to move here after just a couple of visits." Billie and her family now call Seven Mile Beach home and spend a lot of time outdoors and at the beach.

Calista's accessories label, Giggling Gertie, celebrates the grandma figure in our lives. The studio is full of purses, cushions and fashion accessories for the modern discerning lady. "Having my studio in Billie Jo means I can be productive while surrounded by people – two of my favourite things. Billie and I share a close connection, similar passions and a love of fashion and textiles. It's my idea of the perfect setup."

Billie-Jo and Calista are also enthusiastic about teaching others. The two officially joined forces in 2014 and "are diversifying our business approach to include training and support for those wanting to grow their understanding of sewing and all things fashion related," adds Calista.

While in the shop, Billie-Jo and Calista put their heads and hands together to teach others how to sew and become successful fashion producers. "We want to support other creative types to realise

sewing in their spare time or set up their own business in the fashion industry."

Technical skills, manufacturing, wholesale and retail, merchandising and business operations are all integral parts of the fashion industry, even on a small scale in Tasmania. "It's important to us to support the next generation of Tasmanians to feel like they can be a part of a national, or even global, industry." ●

Billie-Jo
Billie-Jo McKibben
20–24 Criterion Street, Hobart
ph: 6231 9293

Giggling Gertie
Calista Anderson-Leitch
20–24 Criterion Street, Hobart
gigglinggertie@gmail.com

Woolstore

Most are familiar with The Old Woolstore Apartment Hotel, offering a heritage-listed stay near the waterfront and the opportunity to enjoy a quiet drink in the Baaa Bar. But few know that its earlier days were home to a couple of fights a night, with some resulting in death. You see, during the 1800s and early 1900s, this notorious waterfront district known as Wapping was well known for its after-dark activities and shady characters.

The National Trust listed Bridge Inn Hotel (now The Old Woolstore), built around the 1850s, contributed to the development of this reputation. From all historic accounts, it was a wild spot. Today you can still enjoy the original tavern area, where you'll notice most are tucking into the Stockman's Restaurant's juicy steaks rather than picking fights.

Wapping today bears little resemblance to the Wapping of yesteryear. Indeed it would be unrecognisable to those who once made their home and livelihood in this most colourful district. The Hobart Town Rivulet has always been a feature of the area, but even the river has had its course diverted. The rivulet can no longer be seen from Macquarie Street, but can still be viewed alongside Lower Collins Street and is well worth a peek.

And the name Woolstore, you ask? The hotel's site was first occupied by shanty housing before it was converted to a wool storage and treatment facility around the turn of the 20th century. From across the state wool was delivered, pressed and shipped off to Hobart's busy port. As the top floor was used for wool treatment, it required lots of good natural light, offered by the saw-tooth roof. This striking style of roofing was for the weavers' benefit and is still present today.

An intriguing wall remains as part of the heritage-listed property which would have been a boundary wall. Still partially standing in the foyer, the wall is one of the few relics of that bygone era. Situated alongside the restaurant it runs from Macquarie Street right through to Cresswells Row. It is thought that it turned at a right angle and continued to the old rivulet. The wall is made from a combination of various bricks from different decades of the 19th century, including convict bricks and many bricks from the old Bridge Inn.

With the original grandeur of the hotel comes the olde-worlde charm and modern convenience of today's Old Woolstore. Where Wapping's punch-ups once played out, now rests 4.5 star comfort, gloriously spacious rooms and staff dressed in smiles not boxing gloves. Come and enjoy a welcome regarded as one of Tassie's warmest.

APARTMENT HOTEL

Hobart City Kayak – *explore the city with a paddle*

There's a beauty about kayaking. The soft gritty noise of sand as you're pushed from beach to water. Your first wobble once afloat. And the gentle splash as your paddle dips in and surges you forward. Yes. It's a beautiful feeling.

From there, you glide. It's a way to see Hobart like no other. And when you do the Hobart City Kayak, it's an extra special experience. Once you've had a quick lesson in paddling tips, they'll slide you from land to water aboard your slender vessel.

You don't have to worry about gear. They have you covered from life vest, to spray jacket, to extra snuggly winter warmers. You just show up at Marieville Esplanade in Sandy Bay and head toward the happy yellow kayaks. We're about to see Hobart from a perspective few people see.

From the moment we arrived waterside we were looked after. Reg has been there and done that when it comes to kayaking – he's travelled the world with a paddle in his hand – and is a local and passionate Hobartian. If you're interested, ask him about his soft spot – taking you to the deep south-west wilderness of Tasmania on a multi-day kayaking tour.

Our intimate group of double kayaks set out at a gentle pace, hugging the shore of historic Battery Point and paddling under quaint jetties. Cruising past some rather prestigious foreshore abodes, we listen as Reg shares stories and fascinating snippets of history that impress even the local paddlers.

On this morning tour, we are blessed with magic conditions. The breeze is light, the sun is glowing and the water smooth. As the River Derwent opens out before us, we realise that today she's in a lively mood. There are classic yachts heading out to race, and the seaplane coming in to land in the distance as we pass the finish line of the Sydney to Hobart yacht race.

If you've ever wanted to feel small and insignificant, kayak over to an Antarctic ice-breaker and look up. Next stop is fish and chips. But not in your typical restaurant setting. With Hobart City Kayak we are tied together in a merry kayak bunch while Reg collects the freshest box of seafood goodness from a local fish punt.

It's an ironic feeling to be bobbing a few centimetres above the water enjoying a meal while a capital city buzzes away around you. It's not every day that a kayak is your table top, and I'm certain I caught a glimpse of envy in the eyes of those seagull-hassled land eaters nearby.

After our snack, it's time for a leisurely paddle home. Taking a slightly different route means that the return journey is equally new and intriguing. The entire trip is a blend of activity, heritage, relaxation and genuine friendly fun. And you don't have to be from across the globe to appreciate the experience, because even for a local it's often the first time you'll see your home city from such a refreshing and special vantage point.

You'll fall in love all over again ... because falling out is not the idea on this trip. ●

Roaring 40°s Kayaking also do stunning day trips to Tinderbox and the Tasman Peninsula as well as three- and seven-day south-west Tasmanian wilderness expeditions.

AURORA AUSTRALIS

HOBART CITY

Marieville Esplanade, Sandy Bay
roaring40skayaking.com.au

Tasmanian Air Adventures – *taking flight on the River Derwent*

A plane with an anchor? I can't help but crack a grin. A plane on a beach, with a pilot in Ray-Bans with his pilot-pants rolled up to his knees? Now that's the definition of a Tasmanian mirage.

We stand on an isolated beach on the tip of Bruny Island, having walked to delirious lengths, which is perhaps why I find this scene so amusing. A plane far from its airport runway, bobbing in the shallows, unashamedly is making me giggle.

As for trying to take the lifejacket demonstration with a straight face, with said pilot ankle-deep in water, this poses another challenge. I look down to compose, glance up, and realise the pilot is sharing an equally large smile. With that smile comes an unspoken permission to be stupidly thrilled about my first seaplane flight.

We are enjoying a quick 10-minute charter flight with Tasmanian Air Adventures, from Bruny direct to Hobart's doorstep. But these folk can literally fly you anywhere, from the gentle curve of Wineglass Bay to the impenetrable south-west wilderness.

"You'll just need to slip off your shoes and I'll help you aboard," Nick explains as he tucks the last of our luggage into the back aircraft hatch. Taking extra care with our nervous Sydney-sider, he reaches out a hand and promptly directs her to co-pilot position. Sneaky lady, I too should have cried "petrified with fear" but my face told otherwise.

We each settle into plush chairs and dress ourselves in stylish headsets. It's time to taxi. A single push of a silver button and the unfortunate crew of six can now all hear my excited chuckles that tumble out each time we bounce over a wave; probably not their choice of inflight entertainment. But nothing on this seaplane is typical. Including the runway.

"Runway D'Entrecasteaux Channel" is in a fairly agreeable mood for take off, and just as we are all getting used to the gentle rhythm of waves beneath us, there is a sudden smoothness. We have liftoff. I've never felt anything like it. From water to air is a transition for the senses; a surging lift, a quiet departure, wave ripples blurring with height as an entire sweeping view presents itself.

The northern tip of Bruny Island, Dennes Point, begins to fade, along with the grand Southern Ocean behind us. Nick kindly veers to the right, showing how behind us the next stop is Antarctica. From this viewpoint it's possible to sense Tasmania's connection to this far-flung continent. Today though, our destination is due north: the bustling waterfront of Hobart Town.

"For your temperature comfort, I'll just open my window," alerts the voice we've come to trust so readily. My eyes suddenly dart from the craggy Tasman Peninsula, home to infamous Port Arthur.

"Open a window? On a plane?" My mind's voice trails off, it's one thing to roll up your pilot-pants on a desolate beach, but to open a window mid-flight? It won't be the rush of air that wipes the grin off my face. It'll be terror. My, did I have a lot to learn about seaplanes. I needed to sit back and relax.

As the light breeze fills our cockpit I realise there's nothing wrong with inviting some of the world's cleanest air into our cabin. It's all part of the experience as the sun sinks quietly behind Mount Wellington. Nick points out the bold Southern Ranges, a cute little dot known as Betsey Island, a shot tower with a protective past and a river-front school that Princess Mary of Denmark once attended.

But the surprises are not through for us spoilt passengers. Following a radio chat, we are told to look to our left. I know straight away that it's not a bird. My first instinct however, is not to assume it's a fighter jet. Coming our way. Rather fast.

"Here we have Jethro, our chief pilot, he's coming over to say hello," Nick calmly announces. Next thing, Captain Loop-The-Loop is turning upside down before our eyes then casually sits beside our right wing like we're buddies from way back. He's endearingly close, and I marvel (while praying) at both pilots' flying finesse.

As Jethro veers off like Tom Cruise, our eyes fasten on the view ahead. The Derwent River spills out before us, the bridge and world-renowned Museum of Old and New Art (MONA) up ahead and a sunny eastern shore capturing the last rays (as any resident will always boast) glows to our right.

Time for a final treat, we career off to the right, flying directly over Battery Point with its patchwork of historic houses hugging the shoreline. We hover above Hobart's city streets, and I smile at the joy of three cars patiently lined up one behind the other at her busiest intersection. The world could learn from these uncluttered streets on a sleepy Sunday.

Touching down on the Derwent River it's only fair that Sammy the Seal ensures we get our money's worth. As if on cue, he pops his head up beside King Street Pier just as we are coming into dock.

I'm not sure what's more amusing: that Nick knows the seal by name, or that the seal appears to be rushing over to greet him with some rigour. It's a fitting finale to what feels like a specially-crafted voyage.

For around half the price of an equivalent flight on the mainland, you can witness Hobart in a way not possible at ground level. And for a local it's equally special.

Not only can I spot that I left my bedroom window open, but within 10 minutes I can be reminded how the wilds and Hobart are so incredibly close. The grand Southern Ocean laps up to a capital city. A desolate beach is just minutes from a world-class museum. And the $99 per person price tag isn't much more than the fine for parking on a yellow line in town like I did last week.

Go one, treat someone special. ●

To book a flight visit:
tasmanianairadventures.com.au
or call 1300 359 822

We can vouch for the seaplane flights into south-west Tasmania too – unforgettable and worthy of opening your window to take a photo or two!

HOBART CITY

Wrest Point – it all began with a honeymoon

The tower of Wrest Point is a little hard to miss. In fact, it's part of the Hobart landscape. But it's only recently I've come to learn its story in full. My curiosity sparked with a simple comment, "why don't we spend our 40th wedding anniversary where the honeymoon began, darling?" said Dad to Mum. I grinned at the thought of these two checking in at the shiny new hotel back in the day; Australia's first casino.

What I didn't realise is that Mr Greg Farrell senior arrived in Tasmania for his honeymoon too, in 1951, and had an instant connection with Wrest Point. Greg believed it to be "the greatest hotel site in the world – right on the shore of the beautiful Derwent Estuary with the backdrop of Mount Wellington". This love of place would be passed through three generations of his family.

The story of Wrest Point is a tale about people, and a vision. It dates back to shortly after European settlement, when in 1839 an inn was built on the current

Wrest Point site by William Chaffey. The site was purchased by Arthur Drysdale, who created Tasmania's first international hotel, the Wrest Point Riviera.

A much loved institution for Hobartians, the old Riviera was a centre of the community, renowned for its dances and entertainment that showcased everything Wrest Point. Naturally it became a much-loved honeymoon destination for Australians, which is where the marriage between the Farrell family and Wrest Point began.

From 1951 on, Greg Farrell senior was the driving force behind the Wrest Point Casino development. He vowed to invest in Tasmania; his view was that the beautiful island needed people with confidence to invest so the economy could match its natural environment and people. He was committed to realising the potential he identified in 1951, and did so as chairman of Federal Hotels Limited. This family-owned company is the oldest continuously-operating hotel group in Australia and second oldest in the world.

During the 1960s, Federal Group catapulted Tasmania onto the national stage by opening discussions to grant Wrest Point Riviera Hotel the first Australian casino licence. The intent of this hotly-debated, unprecedented proposal was to create a drawcard unmatched across the country, attracting visitation to the island year round.

In November 1968, a slim majority of the Tasmanian people voted in favour of a casino on Hobart's shores. Construction soon followed and Wrest Point Hotel and Casino welcomed Australia through its doors at a Gala Opening televised across the country on February 10, 1973. Almost immediately, its powerful presence paved the way for new investment, increased flights, more restaurants, accommodation and confidence in new tourism ventures.

More than four decades on, today, visitors can enjoy a variety of experiences at the iconic Wrest Point, which still carries its local charm and authenticity. With a variety of local and international acts taking stage every night of the week, along with restaurants, bars, accommodation and of course Australia's first (legal) casino there's a little bit of something for everyone here.

Wrest Point is a celebration of the power of community and the importance of family. It just happened to be the place my parents spent their honeymoon. But rather than open a casino they instead took off to Bruny for a few days and later had five children! ●

Want to celebrate your special occasion with Wrest Point?
Head for dinner at The Point, where the theatre of Cape Grim eye fillet cooked at your table and sweeping views of the city are on the menu. Situated at the top of the Wrest Point tower, The Point Revolving Restaurant has romance in mind – only the finest in Tasmanian fare, five-star service and that ever-changing view capturing the city lights, Tasman Bridge, River Derwent and the mountain. Book early and you'll catch the sun sinking over the city.

wrestpoint.com.au

The Gents' Guide – *cycling from the city to MONA*

While the rolling hills and mountains of Hobart are beautiful to look at, they can be tricky to navigate on two wheels. Luckily the city offers an easy and super-scenic ride that follows an old train line along the mighty Derwent River.

The Intercity Cycleway is a long, smooth and safe bike and walk path that connects Hobart with its northern neighbour Glenorchy and leads to the art menagerie MONA, with some great pit stops along the way. So beg, borrow or hire a bike, hit the track and take in some of Hobart's best treasures on two wheels.* We reckon it's one of the best ways to experience our favourite little city in the south.

Start with a spin around the compact CBD, the Salamanca food and culture precinct and the historic Hobart waterfront. You'll find the Tasmanian Museum and Art Gallery, plenty of small galleries, artisan shops, cafés (we love Yellow Bernard for a good takeaway coffee) and beautiful Georgian, Victorian and modern architecture. Head for the Intercity Cycleway entrance at the nearby Hobart Cenotaph, where you'll be instantly treated to sweeping views of the Derwent Estuary as you coast your way towards (and ride right under) the graceful modernist arch of the iconic Tasman Bridge. A little further on is the historic Royal Tasmanian Botanical Gardens, a great stop-off point where giant sequoia trees tower over Tasmanian native plants and the ultra-romantic Lily Pond conjures up Monet's famous waterlillies. Another kilometre or so takes you to Cornelian Bay, where a row of cute colourful

boathouses line the shore beside a dog friendly beach. Pass through New Town towards the multicultural northern suburb of Moonah and stop for a delicious ice cream at Tassie's own Valhalla (51 Albert Rd), pop into the new Moonah Arts Centre (opening March 2015 at 23–27 Albert Rd) or duck in for a bento box and other delights at hidden local gem Kawasemi Japanese Tea House (Dickinson Arcade: 109–11 Main Rd). Further north and slightly off-track is the amazing architecture of GASP!, an art park and walkway that hugs the shoreline

and leads to a stunning architectural public pavilion. Hop off your bike and walk over the water, watch the oystercatchers play on the water's edge, picnic by the river and take in some ephemeral public art. If you're lucky, you might even find a food truck serving up some tasty Creole goodness. Get back on the cycleway and head for MONA, with its subterranean art museum, restaurant and ... well, simply more culture than you can poke a stick at. We like to spend hours exploring here and if we're feeling thirsty we might sample a

ABOUT US

Dale Campisi and Michael Brady (aka The Gentlemen) are Tasmania's travel writing models. When they're not posing for Vogue Tasmania (facebook.com/tasvogue), you'll find them exploring the city streets on foot or bike and generally having a good old stickybeak around the traps. They're always on the lookout for local gems – old and new – and love to share them with friends (that's YOU!)

CLAREMONT

MONA

River Derwent

BERRIEDALE

GASP! Pavillion

Elwick Bay

GASP!

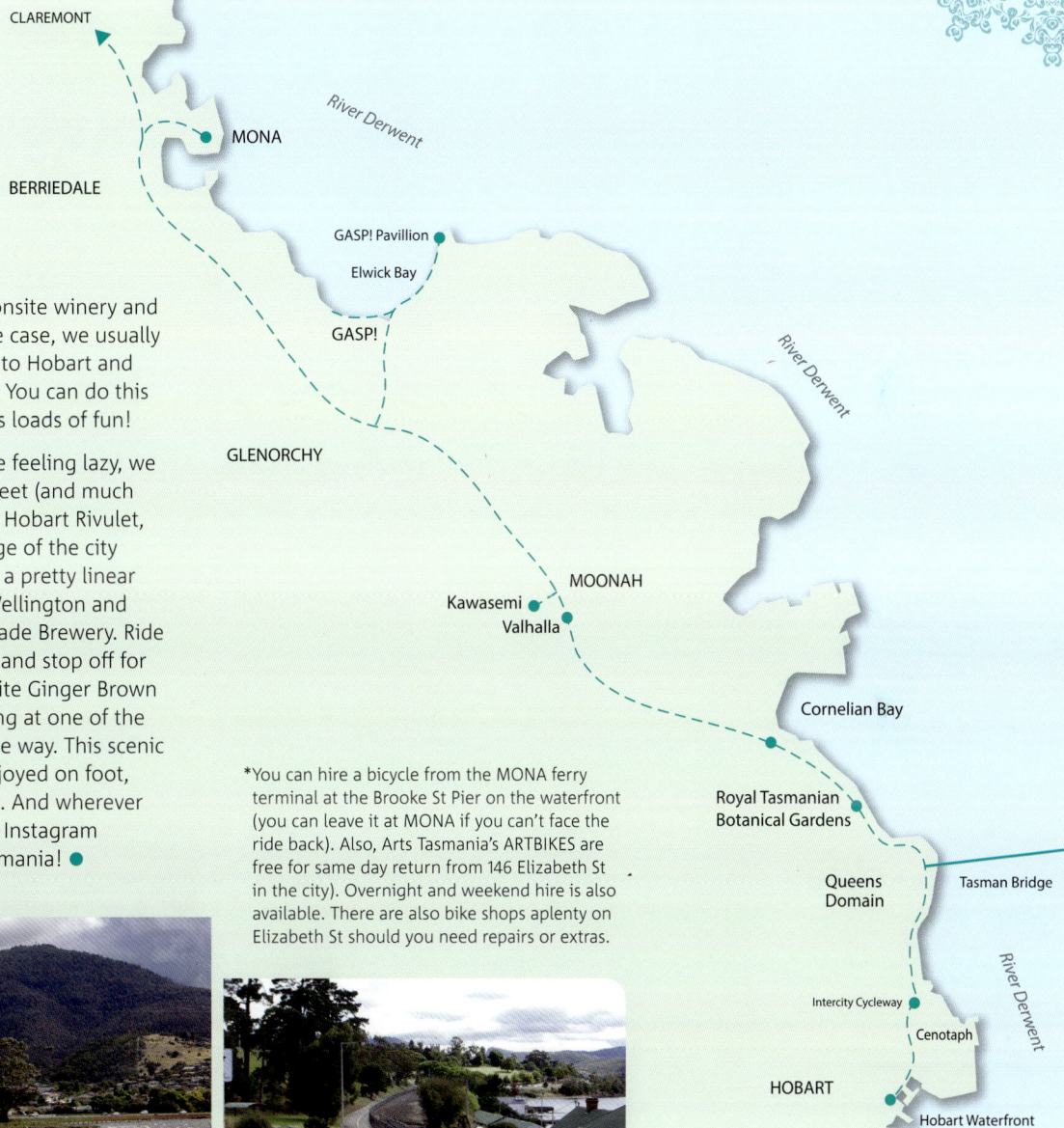

drop or two from the onsite winery and cellar door. If this is the case, we usually skip the bike ride back to Hobart and catch the ferry instead. You can do this too and the boat ride is loads of fun!

Sometime's when we're feeling lazy, we like to take another sweet (and much shorter) ride along the Hobart Rivulet, which starts on the edge of the city centre, passes through a pretty linear park towards Mount Wellington and ends at the iconic Cascade Brewery. Ride back via Cascade Road and stop off for a coffee at local favourite Ginger Brown or do a spot of shopping at one of the vintage stores along the way. This scenic journey can also be enjoyed on foot, if walking is your thing. And wherever you go, don't forget to Instagram it and tag #discovertasmania! ●

GLENORCHY

River Derwent

MOONAH

Kawasemi

Valhalla

Cornelian Bay

*You can hire a bicycle from the MONA ferry terminal at the Brooke St Pier on the waterfront (you can leave it at MONA if you can't face the ride back). Also, Arts Tasmania's ARTBIKES are free for same day return from 146 Elizabeth St in the city). Overnight and weekend hire is also available. There are also bike shops aplenty on Elizabeth St should you need repairs or extras.

Royal Tasmanian Botanical Gardens

Queens Domain

Tasman Bridge

River Derwent

Intercity Cycleway

Cenotaph

HOBART

Hobart Waterfront

Glaetzer-Dixon Family Winemakers – *an urban winery and cellar door*

Nick and Sally Glaetzer (nee Dixon) both grew up in winemaking families in South Australia's Barossa Valley. They moved to Tasmania in 2005 to satisfy Nick's obsession with pinot noir and riesling (something he had been unable to shake since working vintages in France and Germany over the years).

After a few years at Frogmore Creek Nick founded his own company, Glaetzer-Dixon Family Winemakers, producing pinot noir, riesling and shiraz. In 2011 he was named Gourmet Traveller Wine young winemaker of the year and a few months later he drew international attention to the Tasmanian wine industry by winning Australia's most prestigious wine prize, the Jimmy Watson trophy at the Melbourne Wine Show.

Although it was pinot that had lured Nick south, it was his cool-climate shiraz that took out the Jimmy Watson, a trophy that has traditionally gone to red wines from the Barossa, Margaret River and Coonawarra over the award's 50-year history. It was the first time a Tasmanian wine had been awarded the honour.

Nick and Sally have opened Hobart's first urban winery and cellar door in an old ice factory on the edge of the CBD. The brick factory, built in 1948, has been converted into a top floor apartment for the couple and their two young children, as well as a downstairs tasting room and winery. •

93 Brooker Avenue, Hobart
gdfwinemakers.com

Contact: 0417 852 287
nick@gdfwinemakers.com

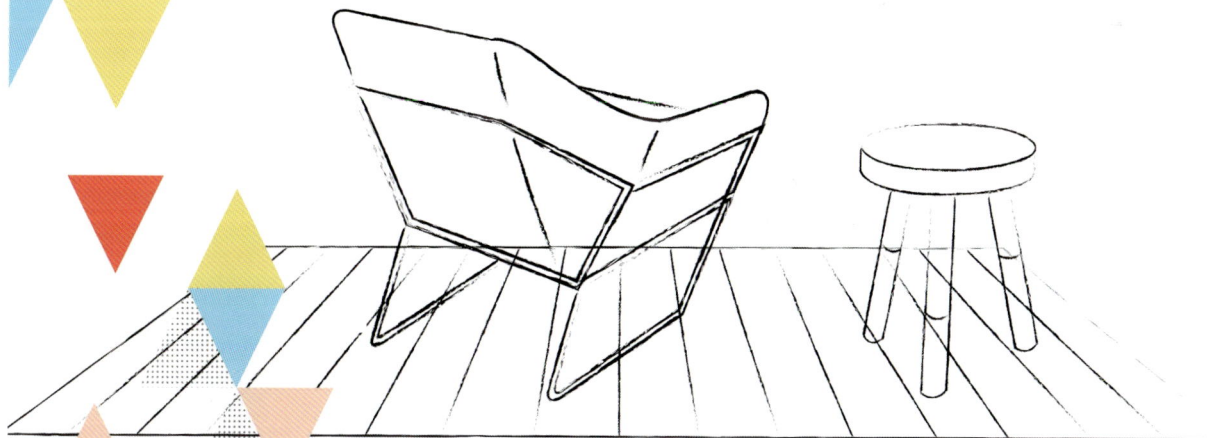

Gift, Homewares & Lifestyle store

Funky Homes ▶ 149a Liverpool Street, Hobart TAS 7000 ▶ (03) 6234 7129 **www.funkyhomes.com.au**

Francesca Collections – *from Tassie to the world*

Salamanca Market has a way of connecting people.

One morning when some 40 of us were lined up at the telephone box, desperately hoping to get a casual site on a bustling summer's morning, I was squeezed in beside Hannah Vasicek. This talented young 16-year-old had a beautiful collection of jewellery and a friendly mother and sister as support crew. The day was filled with smiles and laughter – and as it unfolded so did Hannah's story.

A few weeks later, I asked Hannah and her sister to perform at a Parliament House book launch – Hannah just happened to be a violinist in a string quartet. Later, she began studying a double degree in law and science. In her spare time, she was building her little "jewellery empire".

As the weeks, months and years progressed I came to enjoy wandering past Hannah and hearing of her latest ventures – in amongst a few tired and grumpy 7am starters at Salamanca, spotting Hannah was always rewarded with a cheery bright smile.

Getting Hannah's updates almost became a sport as I wondered how each could trump the next: coming twelfth in the Australian Miss Universe competition, whipping off to New York as an Australian student entrepreneur finalist or heading to the Golden Globes mixing her handmade jewels with Hollywood's finest. I knew this girl would go places, but staggering drive and talent have

taken her far beyond Salamanca. But the graceful smile is always the same and the friendly nature never left.

THE JEWELLERY

Hannah fell in love with designing and making jewellery at the age of 12. When her family relocated to Tasmania when she was 16, she began her first business selling her jewellery at Salamanca Market. Eight years on and she has a beautiful store in Hobart's CBD.

Pieces range from simple sterling silver, to pearls, crystals and elaborate couture pieces. Her bridal collection is well adored and Hannah works closely with each bride if they prefer a custom couture piece.

"I love travel and often design new collections while abroad. When I am in the state you will find me at the Salamanca markets selling directly to the public and sharing my story. I love Tasmania and am so excited to return home after each overseas trip to our breathtaking food, amazing scenery and great culture," Hannah says.

"Breakfast is my favourite meal and you will often find me at Machine Laundry in Salamanca fueling up for a busy day ahead. I love the mill on Morrison for a reliable tapas dinner, Pump House for a sneaky after-work drink and wandering North Hobart for a choice of restaurants for dinner dates." •

Shop 212, Centrepoint Shopping Centre,
70 Murray Street, Hobart
francesca.com.au

Southern Isle Charters – *make it a long, floating lunch*

One thing I love about Tassie is transit times. Sit at a red light and you stand to lose 10 seconds. Want to get out of the city? A few minutes and you're seeing green. Today I went from my office desk to lunch on a catamaran in less than 10 minutes.

This snappy transition from a paper-filled cubicle to bobbing on the River Derwent got me thinking. Why don't we do these things more often? Hobart sits on the second-deepest natural port in the world (behind Rio de Janeiro) with a spectacular backdrop of Mount Wellington. Why the dickens did I eat sushi at my desk the day before?

There's not many harbour capitals like Hobart, and though many of us don't dip our toes in the water on our lunch break there are other ways to embrace our waterside lifestyle. You don't have to know a mate with a big boat (although that's often nice), because Southern Isle Charters is at the ready. They're even docked at Kings Pier, in direct view of many office desks.

Choose to dine on the top deck or gather in the spacious cabin below for a round of cards and a few drams of Tassie's finest whisky. The crew can cater with gourmet Tasmanian fare; there's even a barbie on the back.

There's a freedom in picking a little cove off Bruny to settle in for lunch, or in cruising down to Lime Bay and finding it deserted. A half-day trip to Storm Bay will take you through colonial history, past aquatic farms and rolling vineyards.

My alfresco lunch hour was over far too quickly. If you'd like to make your own memories, Southern Isle Charters can take you to the playground of your choice.

You'll find Southern Isles docked at the waterfront. ●

southernislecharters.com.au

Housed in one of Hobart's most historically-significant Heritage buildings reside several food businesses that seek to provide their guests with a uniquely Tasmanian experience.

The philosophy is simple: it must be local, it must follow Tasmania's four distinct seasons, and, where possible, it must be handmade in-house or sourced from ethical, sustainable and local sources. The 100 Elizabeth Street food family comprises:

Ethos

Set back from the city through an 1820s-built carriage and stable yard is the keystone of the concept and design of the businesses. Ethos is an expression of what the state's premier producers have to offer. Their daily-changing set menus explore the best and freshest of what has come into the restaurant that day, alongside a comprehensive library of house-made ferements, preserves and techniques.

The team works closely with its small-scale and specialised producers to understand the people and stories behind the products, but also how they can showcase them with honesty, integrity and deliciousness.

Open Tues-Sat from 6pm • 100 Elizabeth Street Hobart • ethoseatdrink.com

Providore

Derived directly from a consistent demand for the house-made goods at Ethos, this food store enables guests to take home a little piece of Tasmania through Ethos-made provisions. The aim is to redefine everyday eating for people and recapture the essence of provenance and artisanal, bespoke wholefoods. They emphasise local produce and customised products to enjoy in house or at home. Diners can enjoy their daily-changing, seasonally-derived pastries, sandwiches, salads, house-made drinks, local wines and smallgoods in the atrium dining room, or peruse the library of bespoke rations.

Open 9am–6pm Mon–Sat
9am–4pm Sunday
100 Elizabeth Street, Hobart
providorebyethos.com

Vita

Hobart's premier frozen yogurt and cold-pressed juice store follows the same premise as its big sister Ethos: locally sourced, handmade and REAL food. The team crafts all of their yogurt using single-origin, non-homogenised milk from Mount Cygnet Dairy with natural flavouring and minimal unrefined sugar. With its self serve-system including a counter full of house-made toppings, you can build your own delicious yogurt experience. Vita also houses a customised range of cold-pressed juice, harnessing the nutritional benefits of Tasmania's high-quality fruits and vegetables. ●

Open 10am–8pm Mon–Thurs
10am–9pm Fri and Sat
10am–4pm Sun
100 Elizabeth Street, Hobart
vita.sx

Ash and Besters

Hidden below their ground-level stores you will be transported to a different world entirely.

Beneath us, in all its moody, sandstone-walled glory is Ash and Besters – their version of your local pub, complete with 220 years of history, the most comprehensive representation of Tasmanian-made beverages and customised house-made liquers in the state, and some of the most charming bartenders you'll find this side of the city!

Ash and Besters aims to immerse you into appreciating, enjoying and learing about the fantastic small-scale products our state has to offer. They offer a daily-changing snack menu, seasonal cocktails and a full drinks list, plus tastings by appointment, masterclasses and guided shopping in their cellar, chacuterie and cheese rooms. ●

Open 12pm–late Tues–Sat
100 Elizabeth Street, Hobart
Phone (03) 6231 1165
Find them on Facebook

Beauty and the Bees – *moisturiser good enough to eat*

So what do you know about bees? Tassie has some of the world's last remaining ancient rainforest, where the Leatherwood tree can be found that our local bees simply love. It's an understorey tree of the rainforest and is the single most important nectar plant for bees on our wild island. Leatherwood takes around 70 years to reach nectar-bearing maturity and gives us about 70 per cent of the honey we produce here.

It's from these trees that Beauty and the Bees source the purest and rarest honey and beeswax in the world to make their Leatherwood honey skincare products. Jill Saunders started the business in 1993 using her grandmother's traditional English honey and herbs from the garden.

Every product is handmade from scratch in small batches in Tasmania. They are 100 per cent natural, ethical, pure, and free from animal testing. Whether at their stall at Salamanca Market or in store at Centrepoint in the city, you'll find products ranging from moisture creams, babycare, shampoo bars, soaps, through tattoo balm and beard gloss (yes that's for you men who like a well-groomed beard), and more.

Since long before "organic" was a fashionable word, this Hobart team have been using pure, natural ingredients well trusted for centuries in cultures across the planet. If the ingredients in your shampoo are safe enough to eat, it's going to be great for your hair.

The products made from familiar foods such as honey, dairy cream, organic herbs, cold-pressed vegetable and nut oils, nut meals and fresh fruit do wonders for the skin. Open one of their jars and you'll breathe in the mysterious, rich aroma of the temperate rainforest. That's a nice way to begin your morning routine! ●

Centrepoint in the city, or Salamanca Market
beebeauty.com

HOBART CITY

63

The Brunswick Hotel

Live music, great beers on tap, 33 Parmis and packed with locals – all the ingredients for a great hotel.

The Brunswick Hotel is Australia's second-oldest continuously-licensed hotel, originally built by convicts over 185 years ago. With beautiful original sandstone, open fireplace, cosy booths and recently refurbished laneway for alfresco drinks, the Brunswick hotel is swiftly making its mark as a very inviting gastro pub.

The menu is traditional pub style with a touch of class; dishes include grilled calamari, chorizo and eggplant and award-winning Parmigianas. Great live music, eight beers on tap and an evolving wine selection dominated by Tassie options complement a fantastic atmosphere for any occasion. It is the perfect place for a casual drink, a bite to eat or for your next function.

While the budget accommodation is cheaper than most, it is still comfortable, clean and refreshing. By staying at the Brunswick Hotel you will be close to Tassie's best events and more. It's only a short walk from the waterfront, home to the Taste of Tasmania and location of the Sydney to Hobart yacht race finish. •

67 Liverpool Street, Hobart
brunswickhotelhobart.com.au

The Dispensary

Boutique fashion, makeup, skin and body products and candles ...

Specialising in premium products, this local favourite boasts a stunning range of body and beauty products, fashion, shoes, accessories and candles all sourced for their quality and unique appearance.

Brands include cult favourites Elk, Nancybird, American Vintage, Grown, Kora & Becca. ●

**6 Bidencopes Lane,
86 Murray Street, Hobart
the-dispensary.com.au**

Inside Home and Gifts

Designer homewares, accessories gifts and toys ...

A unique Tasmanian store stocking wares from Australia's top designers and from the world over. Step inside for a divine collection of homewares, accessories and gear for kids ... look no further for the perfect gift or treat yourself to something beautiful carefully sourced just for you. ●

**90 Murray Street, Hobart
inside.com.au**

HOBART CITY

Villino – *fiercely loved by locals*

You could be forgiven for thinking Villino, tucked up towards the end of Hobart's iconic Criterion Street, is just another busy little café. And busy it certainly is, however over the past seven years this petite café has expanded to include its own boutique roastery and coffee wholesale business, as well as a second café to cater for growing demand.

Villino was opened by husband and wife team Richard and Melissa in 2007. Returning home to Tasmania after some time spent interstate and abroad, they brought with them a passion to deliver a boutique product and exceptional service to Hobart.

After winning numerous awards and developing a fiercely loyal customer base, Villino opened its own coffee roastery in 2010. Initially roasting for their own café, Villino has developed into a thriving wholesale business, supplying other like-minded cafés with the same passion for delivering a high-quality product, sourced and supported locally. In 2012 the Villino family grew to include Ecru Coffee – an über chic, hole-in-the-wall space located just a few doors down on Criterion Street.

As well as premium quality espresso Villino and Ecru specialise in alternate brew methods including pour over, batch brew, and cold drip and also have one of Hobart's most extensive selections of beans to take home with you. Staffed by passionate baristas who have competed at a national level, as well as being the home of the current Tasmanian Latte Art Champion, Villino and Ecru are at the forefront of the specialty coffee scene in Tasmania.

Head up Criterion Street, order yourself a coffee and find out what all the fuss is about! ●

30 Criterion Street, Hobart
villino.com.au

CAPULUS
271 Elizabeth Street, Hobart
Find Capulus on Facebook

Behind a roller door at the rear of Bespoke Hair in North Hobart you'll find Capulus Espresso. Capulus serves locally-roasted Zimmah coffee and an ever-changing single origin offering in a hole-in-the-wall style takeaway venue. They are open from 6am until 4pm Monday to Friday and 7am until midday Saturday. You can take a seat on the milk crates out the front and watch people come and go, and have a chat to owner/barista Dan while he prepares coffee for the morning masses on their way to work!

BRUNY ISLAND CHEESE CO.
Salamanca Arts Centre,
Hobart + Bruny Island
brunyislandcheese.com.au

Bruny Island Cheese Co. is an artisan cheese maker in southern Tasmania, owned and operated by Nick Haddow. Cheeses are all made and matured using traditional techniques and are some of the finest artisan cheeses made in Australia. Their cellar door on Bruny Island is open daily. Come in and taste the full range, watch it being made and have a chat with the cheese makers. Sit under the eucalypts and enjoy a cheese platter and a bottle of local wine. Or stay for a long, lazy lunch with a few of the locals. You'll also find a cellar door located in the Salamanca Arts Centre in Hobart, where you can sample cheeses and other locally-made produce.

TASMANIAN WHISKY TOURS
Hobart
tasmanianwhiskytours.com.au

Tasmania's renaissance whisky industry is being heralded for creating some of the finest single malt whiskies anywhere in the world today. Tasmanian Whisky Tours gives you the opportunity to visit three to four distilleries in a single day, to taste up to 10 Tasmanian single malts, to meet the whisky makers and to go behind the scenes of the distillation process, all while being guided through spectacular Tasmanian landscapes from the Derwent Valley to the Central Highlands to the Tasman Peninsula. This is the way to experience real Tasmanian whisky culture.

HOBART CITY

67

eat & drink

eat & drink

eat & drink

PREACHERS
5 Knopwood Street, Hobart

A casual restaurant and bar situated in historic Battery Point just around the corner from Salamanca Place. Inside the cosy 1849 Sailmaker's Cottage you will find 12 craft beers and ciders on tap as well as boutique wine, whiskey, spirits and cocktails. Pick a corner inside, head outside and relax in Hobart's largest beer garden, or step onboard the "retro metro". This retired metro bus with original vinyl seats converted into booths is home to Tuesday night "bus bingo". The menu features simple and delicious fare including burgers, salads, homemade tapas and antipasto plates designed to be shared. They source ingredients locally and sustainability, supporting Tasmanian growers, farmers and producers.

PIGEON HOLE
93 Goulburn Street, Hobart
pigeonholecafe.com.au

Pigeon Hole Café brings to the table a paddock to plate experience. Delve into house-baked morsels, artisan bread and fresh produce, preserves and pickles direct from Weston Farm. Focused on using seasonal, local produce, at Pigeon Hole you'll find a seasonal-changing blackboard menu. Oh and the coffee's great too.

WESTEND PUMPHOUSE
105 Murray Street, Hobart
www.pumphouse.com.au

A whole pig with all the trimmings, great coffee or a Negroni with Australian vermouth. This eatery and bar serves up everything from a hearty breakfast to the whole hog come evening. It's no surprise Westend Pumphouse is always buzzing with locals enjoying the top quality Tassie food, chatter round the suspended open fire, eclectic wine list and lively atmosphere.

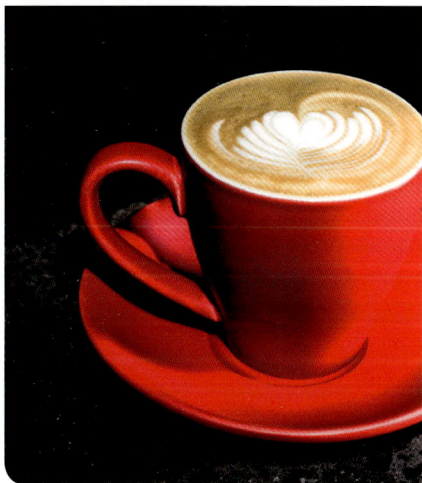

ZIMMAH COFFEE
219b Murray Street, Hobart
zimmah.com.au

Zimmah Coffee is a locally-owned boutique coffee roaster located in Murray Street. Every day of the working week, Zimmah roasts high-grade coffees in a building that has been converted into a hip-café-come-roasting warehouse. There are book columns, comfy couches, roasters cranking and of course, delicious coffee. Stop in for lunch down the laneway and try a single origin or the Tattooed Nun blend, a rich coffee with buttery caramel flavours.

KATHMANDU CUISINE
kathmanducuisine.com.au
22 Francis Street

Kathmandu offers a delicious range of Nepalese food, taking inspiration from our neighbours India, Tibet and China. Picture a quiet evening out with your loved one, in an intimate dining space with soft warm lighting and street views of heritage Battery Point or a lively get-together with friends out in the back room. The menu is extensive, featuring vegetable and meat dishes including fish, lamb and goat curry accompanied with garlic roti and rice, one infused with almonds, peas and currants. The flavours are delicately complex, where saffron, cumin and cardamon marry with black pepper, cinnamon and ginger.

NORMAN & DANN
6/33 Salamanca Place, Hobart
normananddann.com

When you enter the world of Norman & Dann you'll find a treasure trove for the fine food lover. Step inside and it's a feast for your senses of the world-class variety. The scent of the chocolates, the intricate detail of the handmade delights … it's no surprise that most fail to resist trying at least one chocolate truffle. Inside you'll also find locally-made gourmet goodies, beautiful home and kitchen wares – a lovely destination for gifts that you'll find along the main Salamanca strip. Norman & Dann is open seven days.

HOBART CITY

DICKENS CIDERHOUSE
22 Montpelier Retreat, Hobart
dickenscider.com.au

Anyone for a real cider or perry poured fresh for you at the Dickens Ciderhouse? Dickens Cider began in 2009 in Hillwood on the banks of the Tamar River. Since then they have been producing a range of cider and perry using local fruit and traditional techniques. The Launceston Ciderhouse opened in 2012 primarily as an urban cellar door, and in 2014 they introduced the Hobart Ciderhouse. Their aim is to provide a one-stop outlet for all the cider producers of Tasmania. They carry bottle stock of fellow producers and have local guest ciders on tap rotating monthly. They also carry all the Tasmanian whisky they can get our hands on, along with a selection of fine local craft beers.

RAINCHECK LOUNGE
392 Elizabeth Street, Hobart

You'll be fighting the local folk for a seat on one of Raincheck's comfy lounges, but that's half the appeal. A friendly atmosphere blended with cool tunes and an impressive mural make Raincheck a natural pick for Hobartians as well as visitors. And we haven't even got to the menu! Always reliable, Raincheck serves up a contemporary, tasty menu including light café treats through to generous dinners complemented with a good local ale or wine. Right in the centre of the bustling North Hobart strip, Raincheck is the place to sit outside with a coffee and watch the passers-by (if you don't manage to secure one of those tables or deep couches).

CULTURA
123 Liverpool Street, Hobart
culturahobart.com.au

The minute you wander through the door, Cultura's barista extraordinaire will be ready to take an order for your velvety "Di Bella" coffee. Order yourself some breakkie, and Cultura will accompany it with this beautiful coffee for free when you mention Tailored Tasmania. Pick from ciabatta rolls as well as Mamma's home-made sweets. Luke and his team have created a comfortable and inviting city haven, offering everything from traditional pizzas, pastas, soups and salads to meat dishes for lunch. Don't be fooled by the busy atmosphere, the staff will always make time for you and ensure you have a great experience. Cultura also serves dinner Thursday to Saturday – order a classic Italian cocktail and you could be in Milano!

eat & drink

BURGER GOT SOUL
160 Sandy Bay Road, Sandy Bay
burgergotsoul.com

Their burgers are more than just a burger, they are burgers with Soul. The soul starts with their ingredients that are sourced from the freshest Tasmanian produce including 100% lean beef and freerange chicken and eggs, accompanied by vegetables and salads delivered direct from the markets every day. The staff are genuine foodies that will pour their heart and soul into making arguably the best burger you have ever had. Their menu also has gluten free and vegetarian options. Try the boutique ginger beer or bring your own crisp white or beer to enjoy with your burger!

eat & drink

SHOEBOX CAFÉ
211a Elizabeth Street, Hobart
shoeboxfood.com

As the name suggests, Shoebox on Elizabeth Street is not big. In fact, it's rather tiny so prepare to get cozy. Owner Sam is an art school graduate so the menu is not only delicious, but contains "many a piece of art"! Nestle into the Shoebox with good friends and enjoy everything from Peking duck in a sesame seed pancake wrap through to delicious pides such as Vietnamese chicken and wasabi mayo leg ham. Coffee is one of their biggest passions – the barista competes at state championships. The Shoebox team also like to make surprise appearances in their iconic yellow food van "St Anthony" at local festivals and events, so keep an eye out for the yellow Tony!

eat & drink

PARKLANE ESPRESSO
3 Salamanca Square, Hobart

It's tiny. It's humble. And it's beautifully Tasmanian. This unassuming coffee stop is tucked away near the laneway to a car park, from which it owes its simple name. Step inside Parklane Espresso and the sweet charm continues. It's cosy enough to notice that the Mum rocking little bub is popping in to see Barista Daddy. It's friendly and warm enough to strike up a conversation straight away with most of the coffee goers. It's easy, it's pleasant, it already feels like coffee-home.

RASPBERRY FOOL BAKERY CAFÉ
85 Bathurst Street, Hobart

Raspberry Fool takes its name from an old-fashioned, simple yet elegant dessert of raspberries and whipped cream. A touch of nostalgia is what Raspberry Fool is all about. Everything is made on the premises. They bake their own sourdough bread daily and offer tasty pies including rabbit and bacon, Moroccan lamb and chickpea, a broccoli, kale and cheese pie, and Hungarian pork goulash. Daily salads, sandwiches, toasties plus all day breakkie is available. Homemade cakes and slices are the stuff of daydreams – sponge rolls and fairy cakes bring back memories of Grandma! The café is small and cosy with friendly service and huge windows so you can watch the world go by.

BLUE EYE SEAFOOD RESTAURANT
1 Castray Esplanade, Hobart
fishfish.com.au

Blue Eye is a quality seafood restaurant on Hobart's waterfront, cooking fresh and tasty local fish and seafood. Blue Eye has something for all seafood lovers. Try some local Bruny Island oysters or Spring Bay mussels to start, followed by char-grilled fish, a seafood mixed grill, paella or real-ale battered fish and chips. The mixed seafood platter is great for sharing. For the non-fish-eater they also char-grill steaks to order and have other delicious non-seafood dishes on the menu, including vegetarian and gluten-free dishes. Find them under the silos in Salamanca Place.

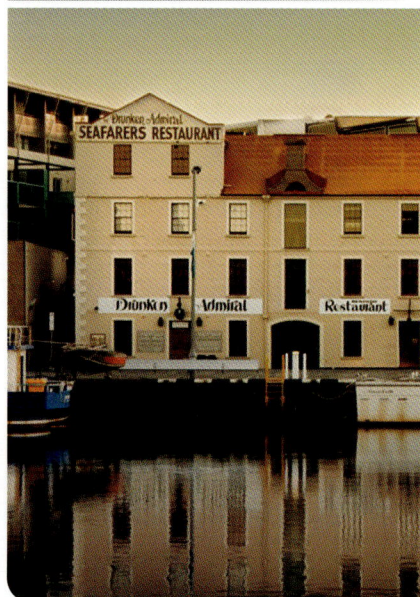

DRUNKEN ADMIRAL
17–19 Hunter Street, Hobart
drunkenadmiral.com.au
Phone (03) 6234 1903 to book or email info@drunkenadmiral.com.au

The Drunken Admiral is one of Hobart's iconic restaurants, world-renowned, award-winning and popular with both locals and visitors to Hobart alike. The restaurant is brimming with maritime memorabilia to delight the diner and excite the enthusiast. They offer only the freshest produce, specialising in seafood while offering choices to suit all diners. Together with their extensive drinks list and delicious desserts, they offer a truly unique dining experience in the heart of Hobart's historic waterfront – proudly showcasing some of Tasmania's finest produce, wines, beers, spirits, cheeses and lots more!

NEXT DOOR
149 Collins Street, Hobart
facebook.com/nextdoordeluxecoffee

This funky little café is a memorable one. The owners got even more excited by the next-door concept and decorated the walls with second-hand doors of all kinds. It's worth popping in just to take a peek at the creativity and fun. Plus, their iced coffee is an absolute hit. With a constantly-changing menu you can enjoy organic porridge for breakfast through to delicious chicken and leek pies for lunch. You're assured a great coffee at their sister café also, the Courtyard Café at the Tasmanian Museum and Art Gallery.

VILICIA COFFEE
39 Murray Street, Hobart
facebook.com/viliciacoffee

Vilicia Coffee is a boutique specialty café in the heart of the city. Sourcing their beans from Brunswick in Melbourne and tasty treats from the local bakery, this bright and vibrant café is a reflection of the cheery owners. Designed by a Melbourne interior designer you can't help but feel happy when you arrive, not to mention your coffee will look equally stylish, prepared by highly-trained baristas who regularly compete in coffee events.

GOURMANIA
Call 0419 180 113 for bookings
gourmaniafoodtours.com.au

Flavoured with architectural delights and peppered with a dash of local history, their gourmet walking tours will take you on a journey of indulgent discovery! Whether you're a local or a visitor to Hobart, Gourmania can introduce you to some of the people whose passion and talent stirs the pot of our blossoming food scene. You'll visit the city's most memorable food and wine establishments, many that are off the tourist trail, tucked away in the city. Savour the best of our cool-climate produce and hear the stories behind Tasmania's "foodie" renaissance. Just bring your appetite!

HOBART CITY

drink

eat & drink

eat & drink

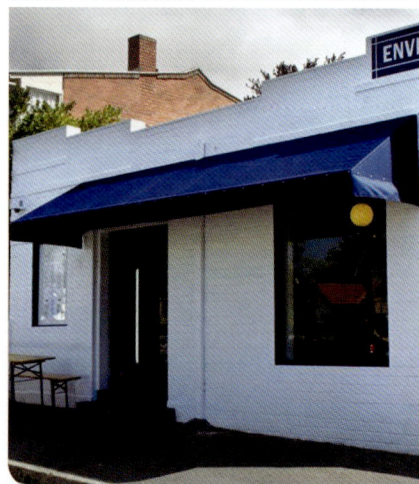

MOO BREW

76a Cove Hill Road, Bridgewater
moobrew.com.au

Moo Brew is an urbane confluence of art, style, great beers and downright confusing contradictions. The original brewery was built on the lush grounds of the Moorilla winery on the banks of the River Derwent, now the site of MONA. In 2010, a new brewery was built at Bridgewater, 10 minutes north of the hatchling site. The architect-designed building houses a modern brewing facility, previously described as the best-appointed microbrewery in Australia. Established in 2005, Moo Brew is now the state's largest locally-owned brewery. The Moo Brew labels display the works of Australian artist John Kelly. Backed by this blending of beer and art, Moo Brew's brewers continue to craft a beer style and brand which purposefully seeks out authentic connections with the palettes of all those who appreciate the art of fine craft beer.

BENTWOOD COFFEE

Anywhere and everywhere
bentwoodcoffee.com

Plenty of people romanticise about buying a vintage-style caravan and carting it off to far-flung places serving delicious coffees. Others make it happen. Bentwood Coffee is the creation of locals Meg and Chris, and as they like to call their 1950s mate, Benny. He tugs along behind them, filled to the brim with locally-roasted Zimmah Coffee, attending anything from the Falls Festival and Christmas carols to weddings and private events. They like to say yes to pretty much anything and also serve teas, hot choccies and chai. It's the type of friendliness that makes Bentwood Coffee taste even more delightful – it's not every day you ask a business what makes them tick and their ethos emerges as "great coffee, having a laugh and making customers smile". Bring back the old-fashioned charm I say!

ENVIRONS

32 Waterloo Crescent, Battery Point
environs.biz

Walk into this contemporary little café and you'll always be greeted with a cheerful smile. Enjoying a snug position in historic Battery Point, Environs offers modern Australian dining with a breakfast and lunch menu that runs simultaneously from 7am till 3pm. And it's not just any plain old breakfast – how about candied and twice-cooked fruit forced with blue cheese on fruit crisp wafers? Tasty offerings blend very nicely with an extensive wine and boutique beer list.

THE MILL ON MORRISON
11 Morrison Street, Hobart
themillonmorrison.com.au

The Mill is the type of restaurant you wander past and wish you were in. Often abuzz with live music and tapas swiftly delivered across the floor, The Mill has succeeded in its quest to bring fun and style to Morrison street. The impressive menu spans from crumbed Bruny oysters with chipotle aioli to braised duck leg, served up with an impressive swag of craft beers, local wines and cocktails. What's more they have a sundae bar to finish on a sweet note.

PILGRIM COFFEE
48 Argyle Street, Hobart
facebook.com/pilgrim.coffee

Pilgrim is the creation of Will Priestley, a young passionate barista (Australian Latte Art Champion 2010 might we add) who is all about delivering great coffee and a menu rich in locally-sourced produce. Take a seat in the 1830s building beside a convict-cut sandstone wall and you'll understand why locals flock here. They're assured of good coffee every time and the raw, industrial interior is always filled with a cheerful buzz. Pilgrim's commitment to high-quality coffee is as steadfast as their food philosophy — keep it local. Expect wood-fired breads from Pigeon Hole bakery, free-range and game meats, and hearty salads.

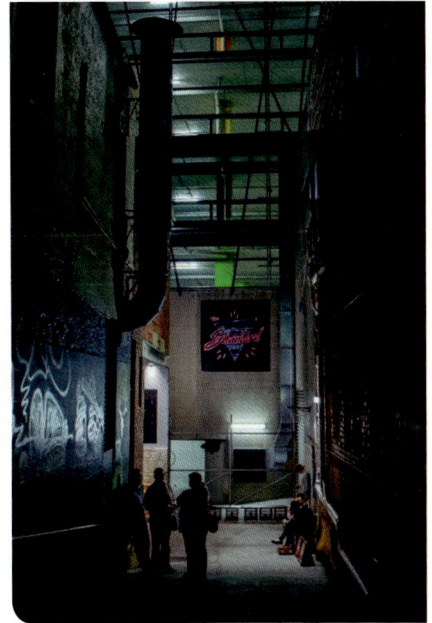

THE STANDARD
Hudsons Lane, Liverpool Street, Hobart
facebook.com/standardburgers

Follow the colourful art down a Liverpool laneway and you'll find The Standard. This groovy little burger joint is all about tasty burgers, served up for a great price and super-fast, seven days a week. Eating in means enjoying the fresh night air with other locals, and if you so desire you can shoot a few basketball hoops while you wait. It is casual dining at its finest but these are no ordinary burgers. Why not go with the Godzilla, a Japanese-style barbecue chicken burger brimming with pickles, aioli, panko crumbed chicken, shredded cabbage and sesame dressing. All the regular favourites are there, but you can also find apple pie shakes and warm house-baked cookies if you're lucky!

HOBART CITY

75

eat & drink

FISH FRENZY
Elizabeth Street Pier, Hobart
fishfrenzy.com.au

Fish Frenzy is famous for its delicious, daily fresh fish 'n' chips, grilled seafood, salads and amazing hot seafood chowder. Pay a visit and discover what the locals take for granted! The fast and friendly service is complemented by the incredible location on Elizabeth Street Pier overlooking the waterfront. Through word of mouth, Fish Frenzy quickly became known for its quality seafood, fast service and innovative presentation of its dishes; a regular stop for many locals. Time magazine is quoted as saying Fish Frenzy has "arguably the best fish & chips in Australia".

eat & drink

ZUM SALAMANCA
29 Salamanca Place, Hobart
zumsalamanca.com.au

There's a reason why Zum is always humming with people, a reason why it's the first café that often pops into mind. Positioned in the heart of Salamanca, its location is as perfect as its back courtyard on a sunny afternoon. The coffee is smooth, meals are always delivered with a friendly smile and the décor is sophisticated and stylish. Bruschetta ricotta, honey brown mushrooms, oven roasted tomato, basil pesto with a balsamic glaze sound an enticing brunch? Well you could literally spend the day at Zum because come evening it's the perfect place to indulge in a Tasmanian beer or local sparkling over a mixed seafood tasting platter.

eat & drink

MAKO FRESH FISH
285 Elizabeth Street, Hobart
makofreshfish.com.au

Mako Fresh Fish is a Fish Market in North Hobart offering the finest in seasonal, local seafood. Come on in and choose a few fillets of fresh Tassie salmon for dinner, or if you'd prefer, take a seat with the locals and let them cook up a seafood storm from their seasonal menu. Mako Fresh Fish also stocks quality frozen produce, and are open seven days a week. Give them a call on (03) 6234 5977.

HILL STREET
109 Hill Street, West Hobart
hillstreetgrocer.com

For over 30 years this family owned and operated business has been a treasured part of the local Hobart community. These days Hill Street is also open in Lauderdale, New Town, South Hobart and Blackmans Bay. The business focuses on bringing the best local products and produce, from local baked breads to veggies fresh from the earth; a range of specialty goods including international products and a selection of cheeses from around the globe; the option of online shopping; your everyday IGA products; and a stellar selection of deli and meat goods – all with a smile and great service.

ATLAS ESPRESSO
2/18 Elizabeth Street, Hobart
facebook.com/atlasespresso

Atlas Espresso is a busy family-run business in the heart of Hobart's CBD. Open Monday to Friday 6am to 4pm it is buzzing all day with a steady stream of loyal regulars and tourists lured in by the great aroma of coffee, fresh-baked muffins and other yummy treats. The friendly team here focus on high-quality coffee, served really fast. You can pretty much bet your boots that if you come in more than once Jono will remember your name and your coffee order – given the fact that they serve almost a thousand people a day, that is pretty impressive! A little-known secret is that Sue here holds the Guinness World Record for most cappuccinos made in one hour (289).

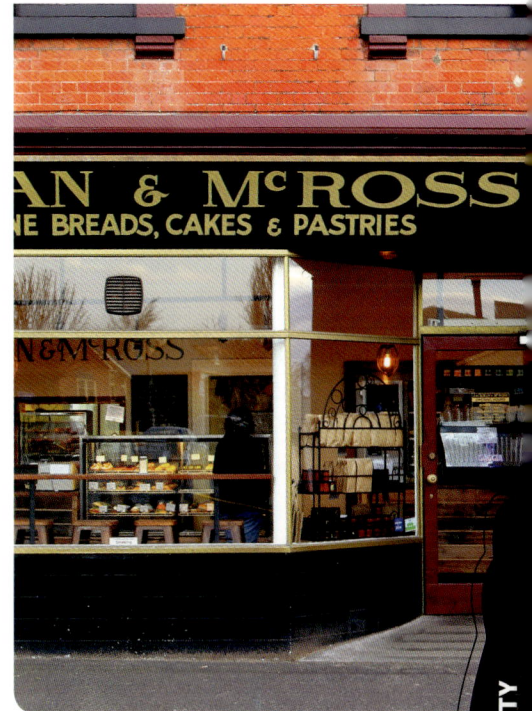

JACKMAN & MCROSS
57–59 Hampden Road, Battery Point

Jackman & McRoss has been a local Hobart favourite for more than a decade, known for its sourdough bread, pies and a fantastic selection of savoury and sweet tarts. You can choose from three fantastic locations: Battery Point, New Town and in the city. Try the award-winning pies such as lamb & rosemary, slow cooked beef, spiced goat & lentil, chicken & mushroom or a spiced roast vegetable pastie, all served with delicious house-made relish. And you can't go wrong with a coffee from Jackman & McRoss – it's consistently delicious whether takeaway or taking a seat.

HOBART CITY

eat & drink

eat & drink

JAM JAR LOUNGE CAFÉ
45 Hampden Road, Battery Point

Jam Jar is a relaxed and friendly lounge with every little nook you could wish for. Wander out to the sunny, dog-friendly courtyard, cosy up in the quiet library by a wood fire, join a communal table out the front or book out the back "shed". Unpretentious and friendly. Expect great coffee – order a short mac, or a glass of chilled Presseco ... by yourself or with a group of friends. Of a Sunday around 1pm you might also catch some live jazz.

APPLE ISLE WINE TOURS
appleislewinetours.com.au

Whether you're looking for a wine, food, wilderness or wildlife experience, or perhaps a combination, experience Tasmania with Hobart-based Apple Isle Wine Tours. They provide you with the flexibility of joining a scheduled tour or opting for a private tour experience so you can adventure further into this beautiful place we call home. Apple Isle Wine Tours guides are well travelled both domestically and internationally, are passionate about what they do, and want to engage you in the unique lifestyle of Tasmania. Apple Isle Wine Tours offers pre-wedding celebration, private, corporate and social group tour options.

TASMAN QUARTERMASTERS
132–134 Elizabeth Street, Hobart
tasmanquartermasters.com.au

You might recognise these fantastic burgers from Mona Market or even Dark Mofo where the crew wore goggles and "torched" nearly 2000 burgers in the first 15 hours. How could there be such hype? Well for one, the 14-day dry-aged beef burgers are incredible, and secondly, if Stuart Addision had any more enthusiasm about ethical fast food he'd be herding us all round the city streets yelling its praises. With a deep and abiding love of market stalls and ethical fast food, this burger joint will have you smiling as you tuck into your sloppy joe or St Peters Pass wallaby burger.

HOBART CITY

T42
Elizabeth Street Pier, Hobart
tav42.com.au

Tavern 42 Degrees South is affectionately known as T42 by the locals. It is one of the few waterfront venues open seven days a week from breakfast until late. Great food, fast coffee, quality wine and an authentic atmosphere. The unique fusion of Australian and international flavours has helped to push T42 to the forefront of dining experiences. Diners can choose to sit outside and take in the sea air or relax inside. Getting comfortable at T42 is easy. Recline on the retro vinyl lounges or sit at the bar. Spread out in the booths and soak up the music and view. Relax after a busy day sightseeing or at work before dinner – anytime really.

SMALL-FRY HOBART
3/129 Bathurst Street, Hobart
small-fryhobart.com.au

Part restaurant, part bar, Small-fry is gaining a reputation for its fresh and relaxed atmosphere and casual, fun food, not to mention its amazing doughnuts (flavours include salted caramel, apple crumble and mint slice). Seated around a huge, steel-topped bar where chef Rhys Hannan cooks your food right in front of you, Small-fry is the perfect place to spend a lazy afternoon grazing through offerings like pork and venison sliders or beouf au jus while enjoying a craft beer or fantastic wine, enjoying a relaxed drink and a snack after work on a Friday, or grabbing a decadent doughnut and excellent coffee from their street bar.

BURY ME STANDING COFFEE CO.
Farmers Market, Hobart

Offering an exclusive blend of locally-roasted coffee, the chatty barista assures every cup is to her high standards and prides herself on remembering your name and order. Bagels are always on the menu: hand-crafted with care, pot-boiled and baked to chewy perfection. The baker switches up ingredients weekly, utilising locally-available produce, including fresh goods picked from their own backyard. Enjoy their delights at the Sunday Farm Gate Market, rain or shine, from 9am to 1pm. Bury Me Standing is family owned and operated and look forward to meeting you! If you can't wait until Sunday, follow their Facebook page for weekly menus and photographs: facebook.com/BuryMeStandingHobartTown.

HOBART CITY

HOBART CITY

SIGNAL STATION BRASSERIE
700 Nelson Road, Mt Nelson
signalstation.com.au
Phone (03) 6223 3407 for bookings

Come for the view and stay for the food. This brasserie just happens to have one of the best views in Hobart. The casual yet impressive service ranges from a lazy afternoon with lemonade scones and homemade jam through to dinners that are in such demand it's hard to secure a seat. It's no surprise with items like crispy skin pork belly on the menu, marinated in Frank's Tasmanian cider. Great coffee, local wines, the historic signal station, surrounding bushland and that striking view – there's good reason the locals head here on a Sunday afternoon. Plus, it's just a ten minute drive from the CBD.

LARK WHISKY BAR AND CELLAR DOOR
14 Davey Street, Hobart
larkdistillery.com.au

Situated on the Hobart waterfront, Lark Whisky Bar offers visitors the opportunity to taste Tasmania's finest whisky and other distilled spirits in a warm and inviting atmosphere. From great coffees and snacks to live country roots and bluegrass bands every Friday and Saturday night, this eclectic bar is a mecca for both locals and visitors alike. Lark also offers a range of Distillery tours, including half day and full day tours.

THE BRUNSWICK HOTEL
67 Liverpool Street, Hobart
brunswickhotelhobart.com.au

The Brunswick Hotel is Australia's second-oldest continuously-licensed hotel and is swiftly making its mark as a very inviting gastro pub. With the original convict-built sandstone, an open fire and cosy leather booths, it's the perfect spot to catch up over drinks or indulge in some superb local produce. Located in the heart of the city, the Brunswick is popular with the locals, who will often be found tucked down the laneway or enjoying a pint and some wholesome live tunes. Stylish and spacious, the Brunswick also offers an affordable place to rest your head upstairs.

ROOM FOR A PONY
338 Elizabeth Street, Hobart
Find them on Facebook

There's room for a pony here, where you'll find a lush beer garden for grazing and sitting back with a fine Tassie brew. This stylish café, bar and restaurant is open every day of the week, serving up premium coffee and a menu with influences from the Middle East, Mediterranean, and Asia. You'll find light and sunny open areas indoors and plenty of "live" plant walls bringing the beer garden indoors. With an all-day breakfast and lunch menu running until 4pm, this is the place to bring your friends, and your pony, for a quiet Tasmanian pinot in the sunshine or an ice-cool cider.

CHULO CAFÉ
98 Patrick Street, Hobart
facebook.com/TacoTacoTas

Patrick Street is now permanent home to the Taco Taco folk. You've probably smiled up at them in their food truck while hoovering down a tasty taco, sitting on a crate by a petrol bowser along Sandy Bay Road. If you haven't done so, you can now find their café in Patrick Street also. It's time to roll up to the bench on your skating crate and tuck into a pork quesadilla, churros with Mexican chocolate sauce or a scrambled egg and chorizo burrito. They serve fantastic coffee and cater for all dietary requirements. They're casual and fun at Chulo, with everyday specials and a handy Facebook page to keep track of where their truck might be. So grab some friends, enjoy cruisy tunes and tuck in.

BASKET & GREEN
179 Elizabeth Street, Hobart
facebook.com/pages/Basket-Green

Basket & Green strive to support local growers and primary industry, with a vision to create an affordable, family friendly environment, welcoming to all. They aim to provide the very best food, coffee and service and it's their dream to create a space that captures the essence of a warm, family kitchen. Open seven days a week from 7.30am on weekdays, 9am on weekends and 9.30am on public holidays, they also take functions and can provide catering. Contact them on 62315249 or on Facebook. Easy to find, they're the one with the phones!

HOBART CITY

BREW SANDY BAY
172 Sandy Bay Road
Find them on Facebook

Situated in Sandy Bay's vibrant shopping strip, Brew Sandy Bay is a busy coffee house serving Merlo organic coffee along with great snack food including panini's, sushi, wraps and sweet treats. They also sell Merlo coffee beans for home use from 200g sizes up. Sit inside with the crowd or outside and watch the world go by. Open 7 days from 7am to 4.30pm.

THE PICNIC BASKET
176 Channel Highway
Find them on Facebook

A few peaceful bends out of Hobart is The Picnic Basket. It's warm and friendly, bright and cheery, and filled with the sound of morning chatter punctuated by the hum of a busy coffee machine. Move onto the menu, and its brimming with locally sourced goodness. If you're not sure what to have for breakkie, you can't go wrong with Miss Watson – she's delicious. They bake their own sourdough, fruit, rye and organic spelt breads in the big bright kitchen and even have their own 'recyclibrary' of books to choose from.

SANCTUM MEDICAL AESTHETICS
72 Sandy Bay Road, Sandy Bay
sanctummedical.com.au

Sanctum is a leading-edge cosmetic and medical laser clinic. It's an urban haven that offers the ideal escape for locals and visitors to Hobart seeking a little pampering and "me time". Situated in the prestigious Salamanca and Battery Point precinct of the city, Sanctum is housed in a private purpose-designed house that whispers calm and luxury. Doctor Asha Ram has over 20 years experience in her field and leads the team of doctors, nurses and dermal clinicians. Sanctum offers world-class technology and treatments that will leave you walking out the door feeling restored.

CASCADE FEMALE FACTORY
16 Degraves Street, South Hobart
femalefactory.org.au

The world-heritage-listed Cascade Female Factory Historic Site in South Hobart is Australia's most significant site associated with female convicts and sits in the shadow of Mount Wellington, a short distance from the Hobart CBD. Women were incarcerated here as punishment, to be reformed, or while waiting to be assigned. With guards, nurses and babies, up to 1000 people lived here at any one time. It is managed by the Port Arthur Historic Site Management Authority and is one of 11 historic places that constitute the Australian Convict Sites world heritage property. They offer a range of tours and visitor experiences.

HOBART CITY

HERBACEOUS TOURS
herbaceoustours.com.au

Do you want to enjoy a uniquely-Tasmanian gourmet food and wine experience? Herbaceous Tours will take you through the farm gate to meet the makers of a variety of food and wine products. Most of the facilities they visit are working farms that do not normally cater for tourists. This is what makes a tour with Herbaceous so different, so insightful and like nothing a visitor can do alone.

STATE CINEMA, CAFÉ BAR & BOOKSTORE
375 Elizabeth Street, North Hobart
statecinema.com.au

The iconic, century-old State Cinema is located in the heart of North Hobart. An independent cinema dear to locals' hearts, the State also boasts a bustling café & bar, boutique bookstore and rooftop cinema for the warmer months. Seven cinemas, from the original auditorium space to the intimate lounge cinemas, screen the very best local and international films. Open every day of the year from 10am, it's the perfect place to indulge all the senses, relax, and be entertained!

SIXTY JAZZ CLUB

The Founders Room, 77 Salamanca Place, Hobart
tasmanianwhiskytours.com.au/ sixty-jazz-club

Sixty Jazz Club is an in-the-know experience for those wanting to hear great jazz music in intimate surrounds. It only runs once a month and they only sell 60 seats in advance, hence the name. Sometimes they have seats for sale on the night. It is presented by Tasmanian Whisky Tours, so Tasmanian whisky, beer and wine is part of the vibe, but primarily this is a place for local, interstate and international jazz musicians to play the music that they want to play. The creators of the event hope this will lead to some great freestyle jazz sessions and maybe even a place to hear a new sound.

HOBART YACHTS

hobartyachts.com.au

Come sailing aboard the 62 foot Maxi Helsal IV, a luxury ocean racer/cruiser. From a few hours on the River Derwent to a weekend away or a few weeks in the wilderness, Hobart Yachts will take you there. In addition, during the month of March each year Helsal IV is based at spectacular Port Davey in Tasmania's remote south-west. You can fly in (or walk) and explore this pristine wilderness with them. The white sandy beaches and crystal clear waters of the east coast and the sublime wilderness of the south-west are Hobart Yachts' cruising grounds.

TASMANIAN AIR ADVENTURES

Hobart waterfront
tasmanianairadventures.com.au

A visit to Tasmania is not complete without seeing at least some of this beautiful state from the air. Seaplanes in Hobart have an exciting history and the romance of seaplanes on the Derwent River lives on today with Tasmanian Air Adventures (TAA). TAA offers local scenic flights and seaplane tours to some of Tassie's most remote wilderness destinations as well as other icons such as Port Arthur and MONA. If you're short on time and want to see as much of Tassie as possible or eager to simply experience the thrill of flying in a seaplane, a flight with TAA is for you.

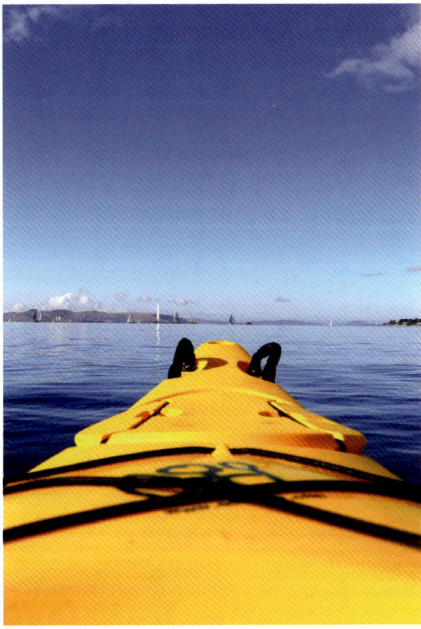

HOBART CITY KAYAK
Marieville Esplanade, Sandy Bay
roaring40skayaking.com.au

See Hobart's waterfront from a perspective few get to experience – from your very own kayak. You'll begin by paddling past historic Battery Point and gliding under fishing wharfs before entering the Hobart docks. Here you can paddle beside luxury yachts, tall ships, fishing vessels and possibly even Australia's Antarctic research flagship, Aurora Australis. Enjoy an on-water dining experience with fish and chips from the comfort of your kayak while your guide fills you in on some local stories. Ask about their Tasman Peninsula and Tinderbox day trips as well as their three- and seven-day expeditions into the stunning south-west Tasmanian wilderness.

SOUTHERN ISLE CHARTERS
Kings Pier, Sullivans Cove
sicharters.com.au

Southern Isle Charters operates out of Hobart and offers guided personal cruises. You'll have the opportunity to design your own cruise, or you can have them prepare one especially for you. Experience the limitless water and coastal activities this region offers – asking the skipper to stop off in secluded bays or get up close to petite islands. Choose to dine on the top deck or gather in the spacious cabin below for a round of cards and a few drams of Tassie's finest whisky. It's all about relaxing with Southern Isles, so pack a picnic for one of those hidden coves or ask for an onboard barbecue.

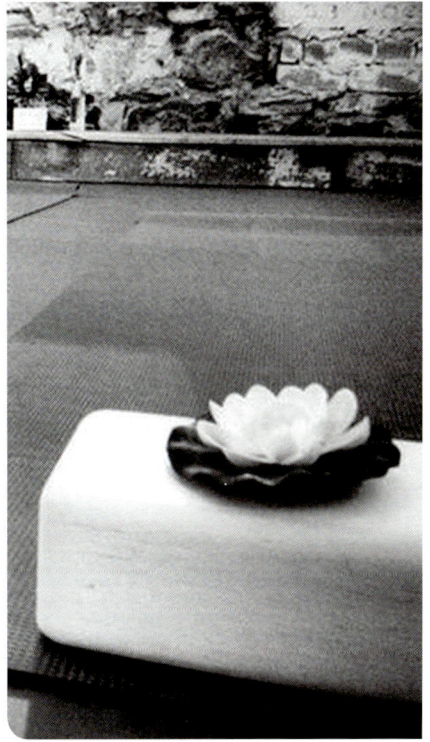

IXL LOUNGE
Henry Jones Courtyard, Hobart +
143b Sandy Bay Road, Sandy Bay
facebook.com/ixllounge

For those who like yoga with a bit more power and a faster pace, IXL Lounge is your place. For this boutique yoga experience it doesn't matter if you're a beginner or an experienced yogi. Allow yourself to enjoy small intimate classes and personal attention from qualified instructors. All classes are friendly, fun and will leave you feeling strong and relaxed. IXL Lounge also offers 200-hour accredited teacher training and wellness workshops, open to visitors and locals.

HOBART CITY

play

TASMANIAN MUSEUM AND ART GALLERY
Dunn Place, Hobart
tmag.tas.gov.au

Since 1863, the Tasmanian Museum and Art Gallery (TMAG) has quietly overlooked Hobart's waterfront. Needless to say, its heritage buildings and archaeological relics are of special significance. They whisper of a past dating back to Tasmanian Aboriginal and early European history.

Today, the collection offers a generous mix of art, history and science with a changing program of exhibitions throughout the year. The museum shop offers a wide range of educational gifts for children and exhibition wares. TMAG is a destination you'll want to take your time exploring. It's a pleasure to know that profits go directly back into the museum you've just explored.

play

THEATRE ROYAL
29 Campbell Street, Hobart
theatreroyal.com.au

Every visitor to Hobart should catch a show at the intimate Theatre Royal. Opened in 1837 this is the oldest working theatre in Australia and has seen performances from Sir Laurence Olivier, Noel Coward, Ruth Cracknell, John Bell, Hugo Weaving, Robyn Nevin, John Cleese, Cate Blanchett and many others. The Theatre Royal currently offers a varied program including drama, dance, music, comedy and circus from international, interstate and local companies. Relaxing in your red velvet seat, enjoying a wonderful show, is a very special evening in Hobart. What's on? Visit the website or call (03) 6233 2299.

shop

BETT GALLERY
369 Elizabeth Street, Hobart
bettgallery.com.au

Established in 1986 by Dick and Carol Bett, Bett Gallery present the work of emerging and established artists working at the forefront of contemporary art. A family-run business, the gallery is now managed by third-generation gallerists Emma and Jack Bett. Bett Gallery has been instrumental in community development through the development of the art collecting group model and it's strong exhibition program attracts the attention of collectors, curators and critics from around the globe.

OYSTER & PEARL
Level 1, 147 Liverpool Street, Hobart
facebook.com/oysterandpearlhobart

This chic inner-city studio is one of Hobart's hidden gems and is a must visit boutique for stylish gals of all ages. Head up the stairs off Liverpool Street to discover this quirky haven which bristles with salvaged treasures and unusual objects. Designer Lou Whiting is devoted to quality and roams extensively to source the finest fabrics and fibres for her exclusive clothing ranges. Handmade with a lot of love, classic, limited edition, functional and affordable clothing and accessories is the Oyster & Pearl mantra.

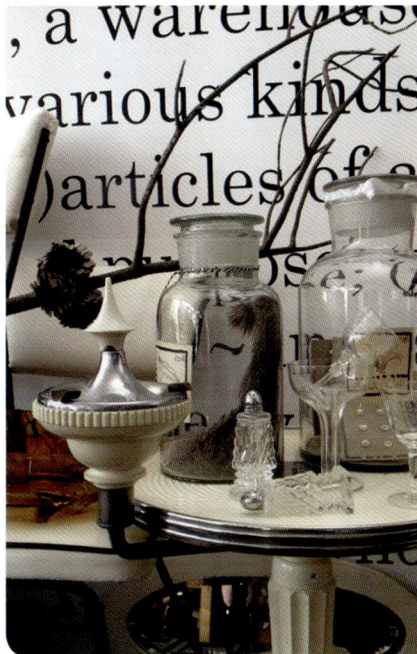

STORE & CO
130 Macquarie Street, Hobart
storeandco.com

Store & Co offers on-trend fashion items beautifully displayed with locally-sourced antique furniture and vintage homewares. You never know what you might find in this must-visit destination store. Uniquely styled, carefully-selected gift items, scented candles, feather-and-down pillows, greeting cards and books fill this historic shop known as the Old Walch's building. It's a classic mix of old and new, which is rare to find in Hobart. You'll find Store & Co on the edge of Hobart's CBD in Macquarie Street. Opening hours are Monday to Saturday 10.30am to 4pm. You can follow Store & Co on Facebook and Instagram (storeandco130).

REBECCA ROTH GALLERY
Shop 8, 77 Salamanca Place, Hobart
rebeccaroth.com.au

Rebecca Roth is a jewellery and homewares designer based in Hobart. Working exclusively with resin from her studio in Salamanca Arts Centre, Rebecca's pieces are handcrafted with passion and care. Her contemporary range includes necklaces, bangles, rings, earrings and cufflinks. Rebecca's designs reflect a raw beauty inspired by the Tasmanian environment. She has commissioned pieces for visitors from across the globe and continues to design exclusive, one-off pieces for clients. Rebecca is also dedicated to supporting other emerging Tasmanian artists by showcasing local art and design in her pocket space gallery located in the Salamanca Arts Centre alcove.

HOBART CITY

87

RED METAL DESIGNS
115b Elizabeth Street, Hobart
facebook.com/redmetaldesigns.com.au

Red Metal Designs is a little treasure trove of home accessories and gifts in the Hobart CBD. It is an eclectic mix of products for all areas of the home, office and just for one's self. Supporting local artisans, you'll find a showcase of jewellery, recycled oak platters, brightly-coloured acrylic moose heads and natural timber laser-cut bowls. Contemporary, modern and Nordic designs fill this energetic space, which boasts a beautiful range of cushions and throws designed in Australia, crockery, vases and bottles of all shapes and sizes. Eye-catching 3D wall hangings depicting deer, fish and birds adorn the walls – perhaps the quirky design feature you've been looking to add to your home.

NICK RANDALL
Phone 0409 098 245
nickrandalldesign.com

Nick Randall is an award-winning Tasmanian furniture designer and craftsman. His studio Nick Randall Design was established in 2004 and is focused on creating bespoke pieces of furniture which are simple yet bold and feature a synthesis of traditional craftsmanship and modern technology. Nick's pieces are conceived on a foundation of clean and simple gracefulness, which is embellished by applying an ornamentation of striking patterning and intriguing details. Nick's work is handcrafted with an innate attention to detail, resonating within the finished piece, each created with passion and care.

VERDE
112 Landsdowne Crescent, West Hobart
verdestore.com.au

Based around a love of design, Verde is all about interiors, homewares and creating spaces. It's an eclectic mix of special things that they find from Tasmania, Australia and all over the world. They strongly believe in supporting makers, artisans and designers from their home state and wherever they flourish around the globe. They have a strong lean towards sustainability and try to support fair trade and naturally-made products that enhance our life, are long lasting, beautiful and practical. They also have a garden store and design business creating outdoor spaces with the same ethics in mind, and their products for gardens are often made from designs by locally-based wood and steel workers.

HOBART CITY

FRANCESCA

Shop 212, Centrepoint Shopping Centre, 70 Murray Street, Hobart
francesca.com.au

Inspired by the natural beauty of Tasmania and her travels abroad, Francesca is the stunning sterling silver collection of designer Hannah Vasicek. Hannah's love affair with jewellery design was sparked at the young age of 12. Eight years on and she has a beautiful store in Hobart's CBD. Pieces range from simple sterling silver, pearls, crystals and elaborate couture pieces. Her bridal collection is well adored and Hannah works closely with each bride if they prefer a custom couture piece.

GREY AND FELT

169 Sandy Bay Road, Sandy Bay

GREY and FELT is a beautifully curated store located right in the heart of Sandy Bay. With a hand-picked selection of designer homewares and fashion products, GREY and FELT sources both locally and from around the globe. It's styled with a Scandinavian aesthetic of simple timelessness. Step inside and you'll feel a passion for beautiful design and commitment to quality that have become the hallmarks of this lifestyle store. Don't be surprised if you end up staying longer than you planned in this welcoming little haven.

ALLY + ME

139 Liverpool Street, Hobart
+ 32 Bridge Street, Richmond
allyandme.com.au

At Ally + Me, they are always on the hunt for the perfect piece. The Scandinavian-inspired boutique showcases the finest-quality fashion, jewellery, leather accessories and homewares from around the globe. Their focus is on classic, clean design combined with the best in natural materials: silks, cashmere, Tasmanian merino, Danish alpaca and buttery-soft leather. Ally + Me is the exclusive stockist of French leather atelier Nat + Nin, Swedish shoe makers Funkis and ethically-made cashmere from Cate Victoria, London. They also stock a large range of Tasmanian-made products, from furniture to ceramics and handcrafted jewellery.

HOBART CITY

89

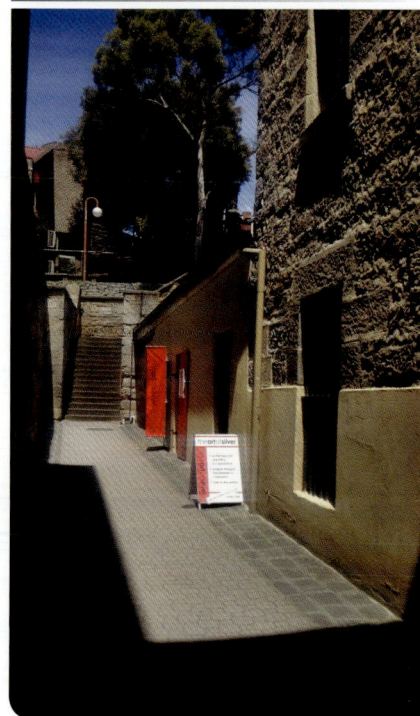

GATHER
166 Liverpool Street, Hobart

Stop in to Gather Handmade and pick yourself up some antlers! This cosy little delight is filled with handmade treasures, many of which are made right here in Tassie. Locals will recognise some familiar designs and be inspired by some new finds. They stock an exciting and ever-changing array of bespoke items including homewares, stationery, accessories, chocolates, candles, hides, cushions, furniture, jewellery and giftware, as well as offering in-house custom-made lampshades, cushions and an interesting selection of fabrics.

MADE IN TASMANIA
25 Salamanca Place, Hobart
madeintasmania.co

There is something special about a product that's made in Tasmania. Whether it's been crafted by local hands or inspired by our island surrounds, you'll find it here. Their ethos is as simple as their name – every product they have is made in Tasmania. Their handpicked selection of Tasmanian goodness ranges from soft woven scarves to fine drops of elderflower concentrate, from hand-crafted jewellery and rustic sculptures to smooth local chocolates. At Made in Tasmania, visitors are spoilt for choice and locals can proudly tuck a homemade treat under their arm. You'll find the whole spectrum of Tasmania's finest including homewares, delicious refreshments, designer art, clothing, food, books and more.

THE ART OF SILVER
Kelly's Lane, 77 Salamanca Place, Hobart
theartofsilver.com.au

The Art of Silver is a contemporary cooperative jewellery gallery situated in the historic waterfront precinct of Salamanca Place. Tucked behind beautiful sandstone walls of the Salamanca Arts Centre, the gallery was first established in 2002. Ten creative jewellers now staff and run the gallery, which showcases a diverse and unique range of hand-crafted jewellery much inspired by Tasmania's island culture, its natural elements and forms. Visit them in Kelly's Lane, Salamanca Arts Centre. The gallery is open daily from 10am–4pm.

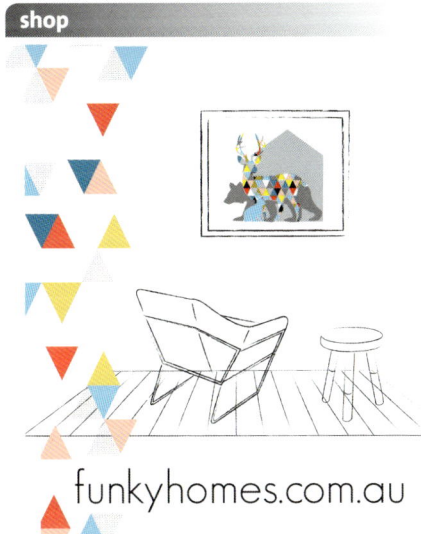

funkyhomes.com.au

FUNKY HOMES
149a Liverpool Street, Hobart
funkyhomes.com.au

A boutique gift and homewares store offering a contemporary blend of unique and modern homewares and gift solutions. Their range is sourced from around the world, although many items are from right here on our very own doorstep. The complete Funky Homes experience happens in store in Hobart, however for those who are time challenged or geographically removed their online store will offer you a taste of what they are all about.

HOBART BOOKSHOP
22 Salamanca Square, Hobart
hobartbookshop.com.au

The shop is warm, well-lit, has wheelchair access, is filled almost to overflowing with books, and is a vibrant part of Tasmania's literary community. They actively support the local arts and literary scene, hosting events and sponsoring competitions. The staff are a small and friendly group who love books, and are always happy to help you find something new to read. They can help you choose a book for yourself or a gift for a friend, and they offer complimentary gift-wrapping. They do special orders for books, either in person, on the phone, or online.

BEAUTY & THE BEES
Centrepoint Shopping Centre,
70 Murray Street, Hobart
+ Salamanca Market
beebeauty.com

Beauty & the Bees uses only premium-quality ingredients found among the healthy gourmet foods you eat and drink. Ingredients like our island's unique raw, unpasteurised Leatherwood honey, certified organic olive oil, certified organic/biodynamic Tasmanian herbs. Only the highest quality honey, nut, plant and herb oils, all at effective concentrations. Hence the products are especially soothing and healing for those whose skin has been sensitised and damaged by years of exposure to chemical skincare products.

HOBART CITY

91

shop

TUSK HOMEWARES & GIFTS
319 Elizabeth Street, Hobart
tuskhomewares.com.au

TUSK Homewares & Gifts is nestled in the center of the North Hobart strip. The store is filled with eclectic homewares and gifts ranging from luxurious to quirky to just right for that someone special. Their passion is simple: they like to have fun. Sure, there's a serious side to their business too, in helping their customers find just the right item. They love what they do, and you'll feel that when you enter their store. At TUSK it's not a shopping trip, it's an experience.

shop

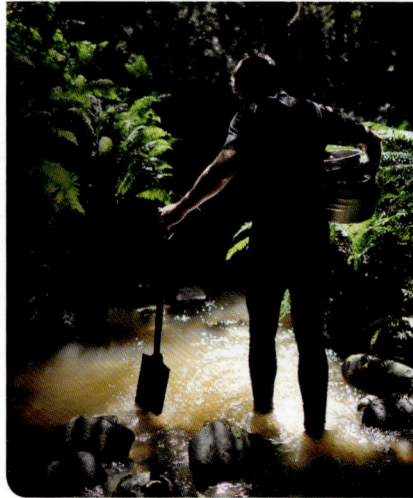

METAL URGES FINE JEWELLERY & DIAMONDS
Suite 3/105 (upstairs)
Liverpool Street, Hobart
metalurges.com.au

Hidden away up a staircase in Hobart's CBD is a very passionate young Master Jeweller, Chris Hood. He's travelled from Madagascar to Burma to the secret streams of Tasmania's north-east in search of gems. You'll find handmade diamond jewellery here – where rarity and quality are paramount. Have your ring made to order, and choose from gem stones and diamonds of the highest quality and ethical standards.

shop

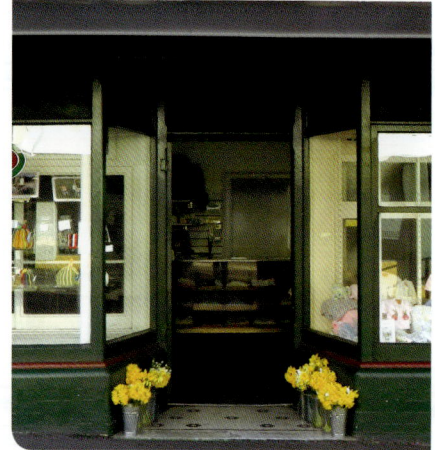

CWA GIFT SHOP
facebook.com/cwagiftshop

Take a step back in time to find freshly baked cakes, slices and biscuits, homemade jams and relishes, knitted and crocheted clothes, toys and much more. They are all made with love by members of the Country Women's Association. The first CWA Gift Shop in Hobart opened in 1942 in rented rooms at 44 Murray Street, then moved to Mathers Lane in 1949. In 1951 a building at 165 Elizabeth Street (built 1840) was purchased. The shop was established for members to bring in their surplus produce and handmade craft items to sell to help them through tough times.

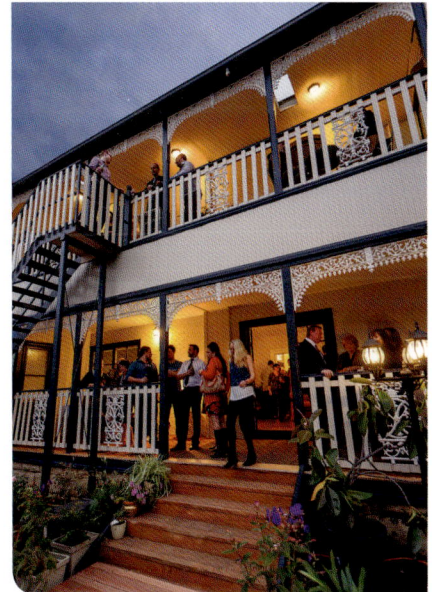

SPACEBAR GALLERY

**Studio 021, Salamanca Arts Centre
77 Salamanca Place, Hobart
spacebargallery.com.au**

Spacebar Gallery is a retail gallery supporting local and interstate independent design, craft and arts. When you walk through the creaky old door, off Woobys Lane in Salamanca, you are welcomed by an engaging space full of colourful objects and gorgeous sandstone walls!

Spacebar Gallery is one of the few boutique galleries in Tasmania which stock both fashion and visual art. In-store, you will find clothing, jewellery, accessories, homewares and original art prints, with so many things to touch, absorb, try on, hold and contemplate. This is the place to go in Hobart for those wanting to support independent unique design.

LIBRARY HOUSE

libraryhouse.com.au

Library House is an exceptional and welcoming Federation home – the ultimate in position and design. It is situated three minutes by car from the centre of Hobart and Salamanca waterfront. Listed by Virgin as one of Australia's top five new getaways, Library House was created by award-winning Tasmanian author Heather Rose and acclaimed musician Rowan Smith to offer an inspirational Hobart stay. Located on wide and leafy Forest Road in West Hobart, each bedroom is named after a favourite novel, with views of the river, mountain and city from almost every window. Library House can accommodate up to eight guests.

MONTACUTE BOUTIQUE BUNKHOUSE

**Battery Point
montacute.com.au**

Montacute Boutique Bunkhouse is a boutique hostel in the heart of Hobart's historic Battery Point, just five minutes walk from all of the cafés, restaurants, bars and galleries of Salamanca. Montacute has private double rooms, private bunkrooms, and shared bunkrooms. All beds at Montacute have excellent quality mattresses, crisp cotton sheets, warm doonas, soft woollen blankets, fluffy towels, reading lamps, powerpoints and free wifi. Montacute also has a spacious kitchen, dining room, sitting room with open log fire, balconies with mountain views, BBQ deck, picnic tables, bicycles for hire, free parking and an expansive fruit, vegetable and herb garden.

HOBART CITY

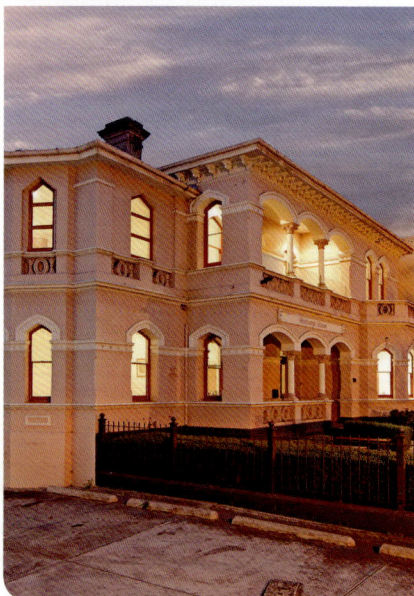

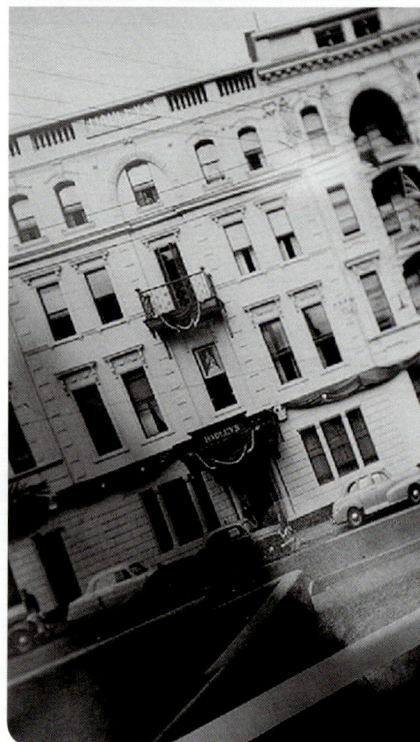

THE SALAMANCA WHARF HOTEL
salamancawharfhotel.com

The Salamanca Wharf Hotel is a contemporary, boutique, self-contained apartment hotel offering ultimate comfort and convenience within one of the oldest and most beautiful precincts in Australia. It's situated only a few metres from Hobart's waterfront, fronting Castray Esplanade and backing onto the historic and famous Salamanca Place. You really couldn't choose a better spot to drop anchor in Hobart. The hotel offers free wifi and parking, with a selection of beautifully-appointed studios, premium one-bedroom apartments and loft penthouses to choose from. Completed in late 2012, the Salamanca Wharf Hotel offers a luxurious alternative to travellers who want the convenience of an apartment hotel.

ROXBURGH HOUSE
162 Elizabeth Street, Hobart
roxburghhouse.com.au

Discretely tucked away behind the heritage façade of a Victorian-era building right in the heart of Hobart is a spacious three-bedroom two-bathroom apartment lavishly appointed with contemporary comforts. Occupying the whole first floor of Roxburgh House, a heritage-listed property with Italianate architectural influence, the apartment offers space for families and friends to savour the pleasure of living in private style while exploring the city of Hobart. There's no real need for a car to discover the centre of Hobart from Roxburgh House. Set midway between the waterfront and North Hobart's food precinct, with five or six minutes walk either way, Roxburgh House offers a truly unique Hobart experience.

HADLEY'S ORIENT HOTEL
hadleyshotel.com.au

Hadley's Orient Hotel was built in 1834 and is one of the oldest boutique hotels in Australia. Offering a range of room types to cater for your business travel, short stay or family holiday needs, Hadley's Orient Hotel is home to Restaurant 1834, The Bar, and a range of conference and event facilities. Enjoy the inner-city location just a short stroll from all Hobart has to offer including the vibrant waterfront precinct and Salamanca Place with its legendary market, restaurants, bars, galleries and waterside festivities such as the annual *Taste Festival*.

OLD WOOLSTORE APARTMENT HOTEL
Central Hobart
oldwoolstore.com.au

Hobart's multi-award-winning Old Woolstore Apartment Hotel has built a reputation among travellers as one of Australia's most welcoming and relaxing inner-city hotels. Renowned for spacious rooms and friendly hospitality, the property is centrally located – within a stone's throw of the city centre and just a block from Hobart's waterfront. Accommodation consists of a unique choice of 242 apartments and hotel rooms; the décor is contemporary and rooms immaculately presented. A comprehensive range of business, conference and meeting services is on offer, complemented by Stockman's Restaurant and The Baaa Bar.

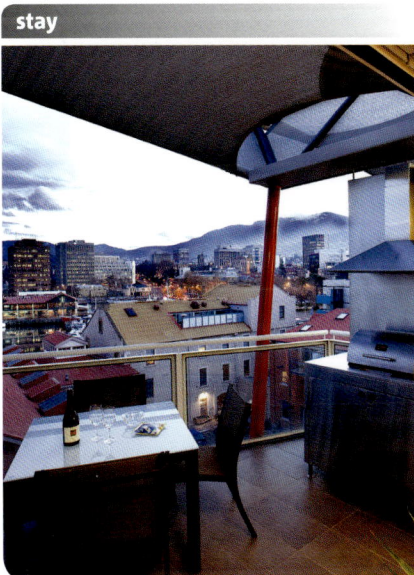

SULLIVANS COVE APARTMENTS
Office: 5/19a Hunter Street, Hobart
sullivanscoveapartments.com.au

Sullivans Cove Apartments is Hobart's finest collection of self-contained apartment accommodation. With 47 apartments on offer across five locations in Hobart's waterfront precinct, you'll find a loft, penthouse or apartment that is just right for your Hobart visit. Stay in the heart of Hobart's waterfront and enjoy the comfort of self-catering accommodation in one of their hand-picked boutique apartments, each selected for its convenient location and five-star facilities. Choose to stay right in the heart of Salamanca Place, opt for a penthouse with sweeping views across the River Derwent or settle into the historic neighbourhood of Battery Point. Their apartments are located across five precincts including IXL, Hunter Street, Gibson's Mill, Brooke Street, and Salamanca.

CLEBURNE HOMESTEAD
(approx. 15 mins from Hobart)
1036 East Derwent
Highway, Risdon Cove
visitcleburne.com.au

Cleburne Homestead is an art-hotel-style bed-and-breakfast in heritage-listed sandstone farm buildings beside the River Derwent, just 15 minutes from Hobart and Salamanca and five minutes from MONA. Cleburne's rooms have an eclectic blend of furnishings. Bold, modern art and luxury bedding contrast with raw 1830s stone and timber. Delicious breakfasts are served in the grand dining room or on the homestead verandah. Cleburne has five suites – the Cottage, the Bakehouse, the Homestead, the Barn and the Stables. The authentic buildings cluster round a tree-sheltered courtyard set on four acres of grounds where geese stroll and alpacas graze.

HOBART CITY

stay

stay

stay

VILLA HOWDEN
**77 Howden Road, Howden
(approx. 15 mins from Hobart)
villahowden.com.au**

Situated on the edge of the Huon Valley tourist trail, nestled on the tranquil shores of North West Bay, is Villa Howden, one of Tasmania's finest luxury boutique hotels. All 10 suites are immaculately furnished and enhanced with a selection of luxurious in-room amenities, including the latest Sony iPod dock, complimentary wi-fi and Nespresso coffee machine. Set on 4½ acres of landscaped gardens with a private entry, it is the perfect setting for both business and leisure guests. The property provides many areas for guests to relax in the peaceful surrounds. It is the perfect base from which to explore southern Tasmania and only 15 minutes from the Hobart CBD.

AT ELEVEN – LA PETITE MAISON
**Sandy Bay
ateleven.com.au**

Nestled in the heart of Sandy Bay, At Eleven offers stylish and private accommodation for you to relax, unwind and revel in your Tasmanian experience. Exuding charm and elegance, this self-contained single-storey townhouse features all the luxuries of home, making it a perfect retreat. Immerse yourself in the comfy lounge surrounded by authentic French furnishings. Relax with a book from the eclectic library, soak in the deep claw-foot bath and sleep soundly in the comfort of fine linen. Enjoy your breakfast in the secluded courtyard lined with citrus or unwind with an evening drink in the glow of the candelabra and to the sounds of the tinkling fountain.

55 DAVEY
**55 Davey Street, Hobart
fiftyfivedavey.com.au**

55 Davey is one of Hobart's original landmark Georgian homes. Built in the 1850s, it has been lovingly converted into two separate fully-furnished townhouses, each residence comprising three bedrooms to accommodate six guests. With well-equipped modern kitchens and appliances, quality beds and linen, and beautifully designed rooms and decorations throughout, these spacious inner-city hideaways give friends and family groups the privacy and security to enjoy each other's company, just like home. With an outlook across St Davids Park, all the treasures of Hobart are at your doorstep; it's a two-minute walk to Salamanca Place and the waterfront.

ARTHOUSE SALAMANCA
Salamanca
arthousesalamanca.com.au

Built in 1880 and steeped in maritime history this elegant heritage-listed house has been beautifully refurbished in a seamless transition from old to new expressing the current owner's passionate interest in art, design and architecture. Individually furnished with bespoke and collectable treasures with generous attention to detail. This private, self-contained oasis offers guests a unique experience of Hobart in a personal, warm environment allowing one to feel totally at home. Step outside the front door and the waterfront area is moments away to explore. Enjoy fabulous food, wine, art, boats, seaplanes and all the major cultural festivals.

THE ISLINGTON HOTEL
321 Davey Street, South Hobart
islingtonhotel.com

This luxe hotel, positioned with stunning views of Mount Wellington, is nestled away at the top of Davey Street in South Hobart. With a commitment to personal service, fine art and meticulously appointed rooms, Islington is the type of place that's hard to leave for a day's exploring. Islington is a hotel of stories. Corridors and rooms showcase an eclectic mix of ancient and modern art, antiques and objects d'art collected over 30 years of world travels and enhanced by the owner's family history in Tasmania. Guest rooms are sumptuously furnished and reflect a rich Tasmanian history. In the guest-only restaurant, the resident chef's focus is always seasonal, local and organic where possible.

THE HENRY JONES ART HOTEL
2/19a Hunter Street, Hobart
thehenryjones.com

The Henry Jones Art Hotel is located on Hobart's waterfront and is Australia's first dedicated art hotel. The site dates back to 1804 and the former jam factory has been transformed into an enthralling first-class hotel designed by award-winning architects, Morris-Nunn & Associates. The hotel is furnished with over 500 artworks and presents an environment in which people can experience art in a new and more immediate way. With a continually-changing exhibition, the hotel has been created to present itself as a fusion of art, heritage, tradition and nature. Exterior and interior spaces present art as part of the Hotel's function and beauty.

HOBART CITY

kunanyi / Mt Wellington

What the locals love

TIPS FROM THOSE WHO LIVE HERE
kunanyi/Mount Wellington area

> They're called secret falls for a reason. But if you go poking about up around the foothills of Mount Wellington you might stumble across them.

> Walk to Junction Cabin with a thermos of hot chocolate to enjoy at the cabin.

> For a steep climb worth the effort, the walk to Cathedral Rock is one of the best on the mountain.

> The Point to Pinnacle (held in Nov) is the only half-marathon in Australia where you can see the start from the finish and the finish from the start. Beginning at Wrest Point, you'll feel on top of the world when you make it to the top of Mount Wellington.

KUNANYI/MT WELLINGTON

> Enjoy a bike ride? The North-South Track connects Mount Wellington Springs to the Glenorchy Mountain Bike Track. Log rides and jumps are scattered throughout for the daring peeps and rock scree sections create nice variation from the forested sections. Alternatively, the Pipeline Track is a little less challenging, beginning at Fern Tree and winding through cool forest up to Neika. Some locals leave their bikes here and continue on foot along the Wellington Falls Track to the lookout.

> Explore the site of the former Springs Hotel, destroyed in the 1967 bushfires, that became known as "Hobart's pub with no beer".

Derwent Valley

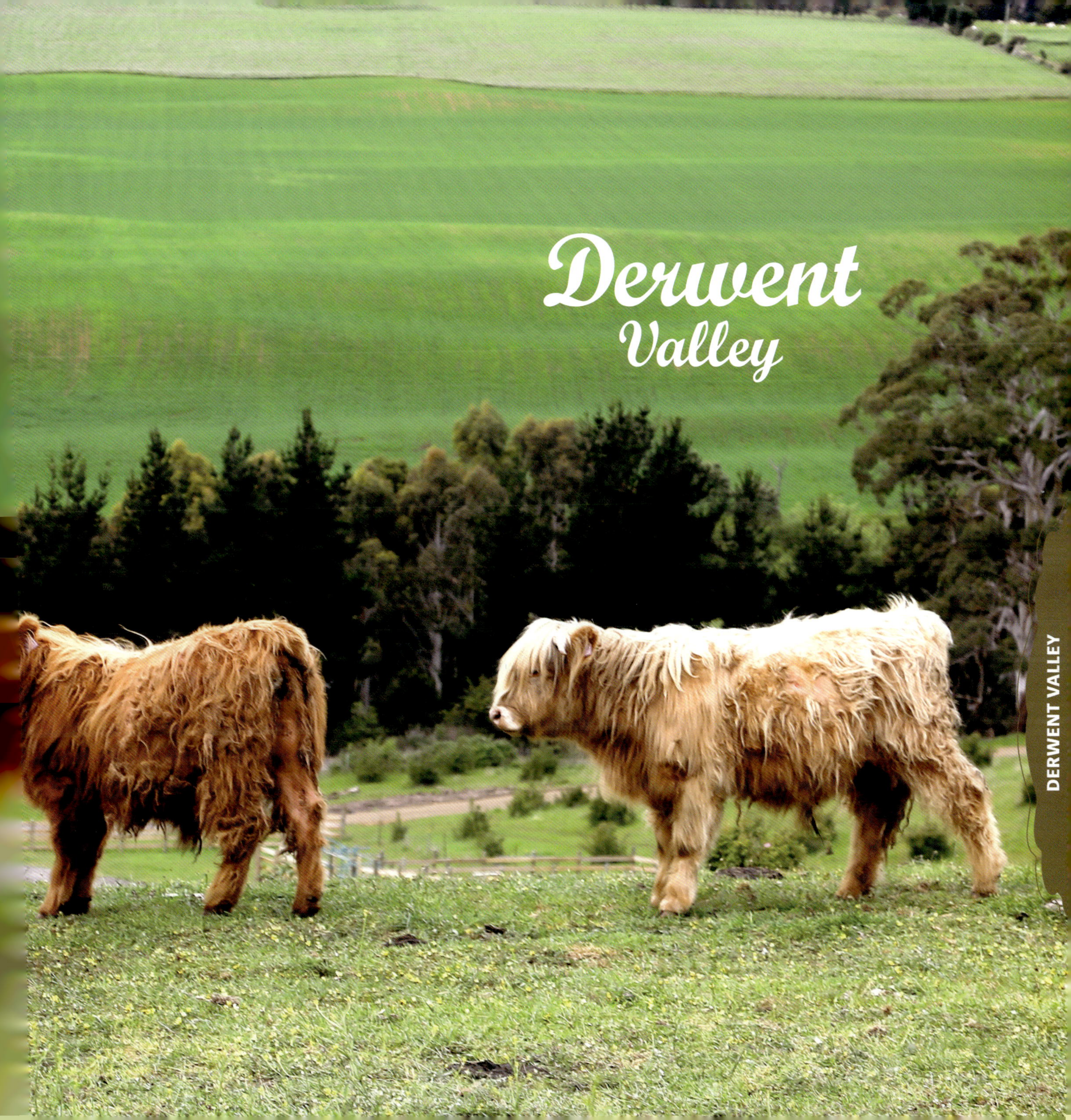

TIPS FROM THOSE WHO LIVE HERE
Derwent Valley

DERWENT VALLEY

> Take the tall trees walk at Mount Field and on your way back be sure to reward yourself with an ale in the paddock at Two Metre Tall's Farm Bar. It's not often you can enjoy a cider or beer made in small batches and poured by a two-metre tall man. Most ingredients are direct from the farm, or sourced from Tassie farmers nearby.

> Poke around the antique shops and explore Willow Court.

> The Possum Shed at Westerway is well worth seeking out.

> Camping at the Government Huts Mt Field for about $10 a night is a great experience. During autumn/winter you travel through the foggy Derwent Valley then drive up the mountain above the clouds. It's also a great place to see some "fagus" and has some incredible star gazing.

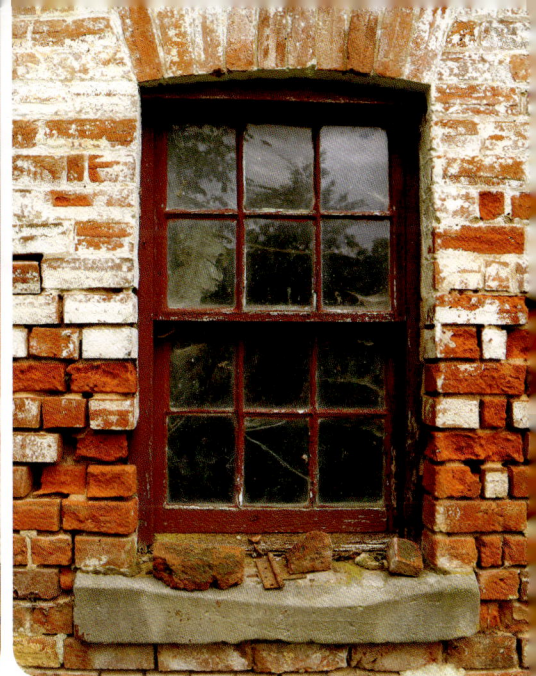

Derwent Valley Discovering

"I reckon I'm the luckiest girl in the Valley," says Bec with a proud grin.
"From where I stand, I can see the point of Mount Wellington and the snow on Mount Field."

We're standing in the middle of a paddock in the Derwent Valley. I'd never met Bec until I casually asked one of her neighbours, Ashley, where I could find "some of those shaggy-looking cows".

A big grin appeared on Ashley's face as he whipped out his phone and told me he knew just the lady to help. She lived just over the river, and even if she wasn't home I could still jump her fence and go looking for her prized highland cattle. She wouldn't mind.

Turns out Bec is a former Valley girl herself, who lived many years away before returning to her home patch where she has about 50 of these beauties and plans to build her home.

Ashley Huntington and wife Jane are equally fond of the Valley, and although

I spend a few short hours meeting the locals and discovering what lies behind unmarked farm gates, I realise there's lots more to this region than a road to elsewhere. It's filled with characters and the kind of surrounds that beg you to stay longer than planned.

As tall as the fellow himself, Ashley's Two Metre Tall Brewery is a pretty special 600-hectare haven. There's Black Angus cows and Wagyu cows and chickens and pigs and, believe it or not, also a bar in the paddock.

Here, Ashley will pour you an ale or cider from farm-grown ingredients – a true paddock to hand-pumped pint experience. They grow grain and hops, and Ashley puts his organic chemistry degree to work in a way that brings much happiness to visitors of

the Valley. Beer-fed beef can also be purchased at the brewery, and they're most happy for you to bring a picnic.

Just up the road, there's even more surprises in store. It just so happens there's convict buildings a good 12 years older than those of Port Arthur. What's more, they come with a fine dram of single-malt whisky.

No sooner have we arrived at Redlands Estate than we are whisked around the corner in the whisky bar to the "smelling room", where wooden plugs are pulled from three hefty barrels. It's a sensory welcome about as intriguing as the newly-bottled apple schnapps that comes complete with a bobbing apple.

Redlands has a good bit of history. It was granted to George Frederick Read, an

outcast son of King George IV of England, and was the location of bushranger hold-ups and much more. So much more, we decide to wander the three-hectare gardens to contemplate its past.

We wander over cobblestones to an old wooden door – push it open – walk through a dimly-lit outhouse and out into the bright light. There before us, of all things, is a full-length clay tennis court lined with flowers.

There's lush green surrounds that tumble down to the river's edge where the sound of water tumbling across rocks adds to the whimsical setting. It's like a fairy tale, a hidden garden that only the royals of the time might play in. There's even a swing in the sunshine.

Next door are the Salmon Ponds, the heritage trout hatchery where our very first trout were raised in 1864 – the first in the southern hemisphere. Those who love hooking a rainbow or brown trout here in Tassie, like my uncle, have much to be thankful for to the men who carefully reared these babies. In doing so, they hatched a beloved pastime.

Talking of years gone by, New Norfolk is also the place to go if you're after something beautifully old. Speciality antique stores are sprinkled through the town like little windows into the past. The Drill Hall Emporium is so tastefully displayed you'd think that someone from 1873 is far more stylish than any of us could attempt to be. Dining tables whisper secrets, rolling pins tell of hard-working palms and suitcases hold tales of long-gone journeys.

Speaking of journeys, some people were sent to New Norfolk to get psychiatric

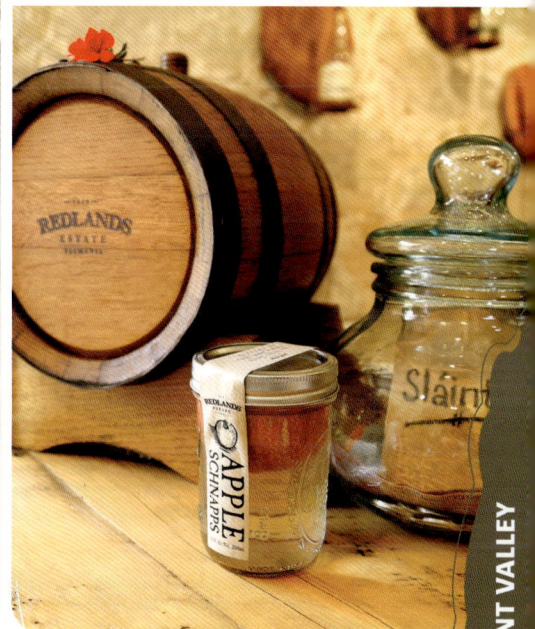

help. The former psychiatric hospital has been transformed into little stores featuring antiques and collectibles. Willow Court Antique Centre, the quaint Patchwork Café, boats under willows, outdoor pianos, dilapidated buses … for me the area cast a rather intriguing spell.

Now, I've barely told half the tale of my day in the Valley and there's one thing I've realised for certain. One day isn't enough. Not even two or three perhaps. We didn't even start on the vineyards,

nor the wall in the wilderness or that gorgeous Russell Falls. So, it's important to find a place to rest your head.

There's one you can stay in that may just have you feeling like royalty, an 1825 convict-built mansion. Is it because you can pluck an apricot straight from the tree on arrival or you can see a hand-written name that convict "Lewis" wrote in chalk on the staircase? Or is it because it overlooks the gorgeous River Derwent? I'm not sure what it is about Woodbridge

on the Derwent that makes it feel so luxurious, so regal. What I do know is that when you walk through its doors, you feel at home. You feel enveloped in charm, you feel its walls want to share a distant past, and simultaneously you are indulged in modern luxury. Although it boasts 39 rooms, only 16 guests at a time get to enjoy Woodbridge. ●

Words and images by Alice Hansen

Woodbridge on the Derwent

"Yes, I think we can save it! But what the hell would we do with it?" asked John.

It was 2004, and Laurelle and John Grimley were standing on the roadside looking at one of the oldest buildings in Australia, the derelict mansion, Woodbridge, built in 1825 on the riverfront at Elizabeth Town (now New Norfolk), the first "capital" of the fledgling Van Diemens Land.

"I don't know, " said Laurelle, "but I know that if I don't grab this, I will never get the chance to do something like it again."

Hence began what has been an 11-year labour of love (well most days, at least!)

Two years later Woodbridge won the 2005 HIA Tasmanian Renovation of the Year, and then took out the 2006 Australian award. "Woodbridge was in a bad way," said John. "Restoring it made 'Grand Designs' and 'The Block' look like a walk in the park."

"But saving her was only part of the equation," said Laurelle. "If she (she has always been a lady to me!) was to survive, she had to pay her way. We had to find a productive use for her that would make her continued survival an economic proposition. Inspired by 'Pride and Prejudice', 'Regency House Party', 'Duchess of Duke Street' and, dare we say a healthy smattering of 'Fawlty Towers', we decided to run Woodbridge as a luxury boutique hotel."

"The following years establishing 'Woodbridge' as 'Woodbridge on the Derwent', Small Luxury Hotel, required sustained hard work and dedication," said John. "Our ambition to turn Woodbridge into Tasmania's, indeed Australia's, pre-eminent historic luxury accommodation has, in turn, made the restoration itself look like a walk in the park," he explained. "But she warrants the effort – there is nothing else quite like Woodbridge anywhere in Australia!"

1825

DERWENT VALLEY

eat & drink

eat & drink

play

play

THE PATCHWORK CAFÉ
15 George Street, New Norfolk
patchworkcafe.com.au

The Patchwork Café is a cosy little café housed in an old chapel, in the grounds of historical Willow Court. The café serves award-winning coffees as well as their famous OMG burgers and specialty homemade pies, sweet treats and more. Set in manicured gardens with outdoor eating space, you can bring your four-legged friend along also. On Sunday afternoons, relax under a tree with a glass of wine and take in the smooth sounds of live jazz (warmer months). With cheerful staff and daily specials, Patchwork Café is open seven days and offers gluten-free and vegetarian options. Call 0417 916 479 or find the café on Facebook.

TWO METRE TALL
FARM BAR & BREWERY
2862 Lyell Highway, Hayes
2mt.com.au

Visit the Two Metre Tall Farm Bar in the stunning Derwent Valley to experience the fierce independence of this farmer and fermenter! His mission is to return beer from the "wasteland of industrial brewing" to its true origins as an agricultural food of unparalleled history, diversity and flavour. The Two Metre Tall brewery exclusively produces Farmhouse Ale and Cider from ingredients they grow (grain and hops) or procure directly from Tasmanian farmers. They also grow Black Angus/Wagyu beef and you can cook one of their steaks on the BBQ while enjoying a pint of hand-pumped ale or cider at the Farm Bar. Head online to purchase interesting special release brews only available direct.

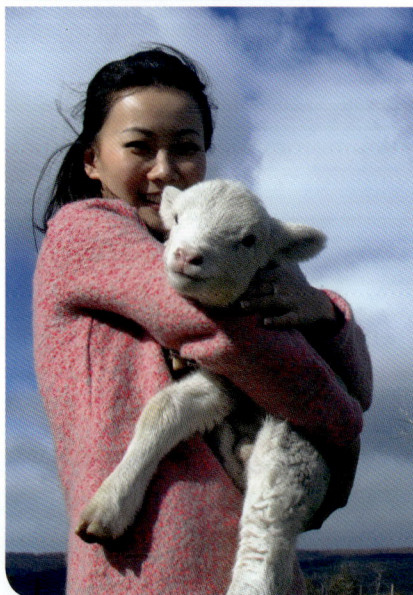

CURRINGA FARM
5831 Lyell Highway, Hamilton
curringafarm.com.au

Open daily, September to April, from 10.00am. Bookings are essential, phone 0418 863 337

Curringa Farm is a sixth-generation farmstay and tour attraction giving visitors a taste of country life on a real 750 acre working farm. Learn about wool production, sheep husbandry and cropping activities. Beautiful self-contained spa cottages with decks and gas BBQs overlook picturesque Lake Meadowbank. See best-practice landcare and farming techniques. Enjoy a delicious BBQ lunch for a minimum of six people or the Shearers Smoko for a minimum of four. Includes sheep shearing, working farm dogs, crops in season and a conservation forest walk.

REDLANDS ESTATE DISTILLERY

Along with producing some of the finest hand-crafted single malt whisky in Australia, Redlands Estate Distillery is also one of Tasmania's oldest and more interesting heritage properties. Granted to the outcast son of King George IV of England in 1819, Redlands was one of the most productive of Australia's hop farms until the 1970s. The farm had its own cobblestone village including bakery, shop, butcher and bell tower to service the 200 local workers and their families on the farm. Today Redlands Estate is one of only two "paddock to bottle" single malt whisky distilleries in the world. Located a short drive from New Norfolk, tours of the distillery are available and you can also go for the option of a self-guided tour through the extensive gardens before stopping for a taste at the cellar door.

DERWENT VALLEY

Huon Valley

TIPS FROM THOSE WHO LIVE HERE

Huon Valley

> Hunt for fossils at Drip Beach, just beyond Cygnet. The calm here will stop you in your tracks.

> There's a waterhole. It's so gorgeous and so special to us that we can't bring ourselves to give the exact location. But we will say it's on the way to Huonville, about 20 minutes from the city centre and you'll find wild berries to eat when you get close.

> Watch the craftsmen down at the boat building school in Franklin – there's a fantastic museum at the Australian Antarctic Division that's free and well worth a peek on your way south.

> Hidden away in Cygnet you'll find a gorgeous destination for Sunday Lunch. The Red Velvet Lounge is home to a former Country Chef of the Year – let Steve Cumper treat you to a long relaxed lunch.

> Walk the Kaoota Tramway Track – an old trail that led from Margate to a coal mine in Kaoota. There's also a fantastic heritage museum at Margate and little ones are quite partial to visiting the Margate Train and choosing lollies at the lolly shop. For the big kids there's great coffee at a nearby church-turned-quaint-café aptly named Heavens Above.

> Lay out a picnic at the beach at Middleton.

> You can't drive any further south in Australia than Cockle Creek. What you'll find there and along the way is pretty special.

> Geeveston happens to be home to some spectacular sushi. You'll also find Masaaki at the farmer's market in the city each Sunday.

Heading south on a Sunday Afternoon

Still infused with laziness, it's not easy to write through this relaxed haze. But surely this is what Sundays in Tassie are all about. Hop in the car and head south if you're feeling in need of some time set aside just for you in surrounds that'll make you want to grab a blankie from The Apple Shed's blankie supply box and have a good nap after lunch.

That's right, first stop is The Apple Shed Museum and Ciderhouse, home to Willie Smith cider just 30 minutes drive from Hobart. This rustic 1942 apple shed is filled with history, artisan ciders and a good dose of locally-sourced food.

I sit back in the barn, feeling slightly nostalgic, as my grandmother used to talk of her days in Cygnet, at a time when the apple industry boomed. More than once dear 90-something-year-old Madge spoke fondly of the time she was "chaperone to the Apple Queen". I'm guessing this included plenty of nose powdering, but at the time it was a highly-sought position that even involved a journey to distant Queensland. I think Grandma would have loved to wander this museum filled with photos of notable "apple men", sorting machines and every apple variety you could imagine neatly rowed in alphabetical order.

Lunch out in the barn is the countryside's answer for a relaxing Sunday. A seasonal, sustainable menu is served up, showcasing produce from passionate local growers. A Pigeon Hole sourdough toastie, generously plump with goats cheese, beetroot and rocket takes my fancy and of course the menu offers plenty of refreshing accompaniments, starting with cider.

Pleasantly full, wander the museum then on the way home if you're feeling adventurous stop off for a swim in the most exquisite of waterholes. It wouldn't be fair to give its exact location, but if you're lucky a friendly local will point you in the right direction. Let's just say it's an invigorating local secret that sometimes you'll have entirely to yourself. Leap off the rock, or sit by the bubbling stream that fills the waterhole with cool mountain water.

This place will make you feel like you're at your Nanna's, but also that she's suddenly become incredibly hip. In fact,

there might be a local Nan or two sitting on the vintage chair beside you. You'll see by her smile that she's pretty happy that her era is trending here in Margate.

Beautiful apple pie with a dollop of cream, rich aromas of coffee, you can even fill your tea cup with a creative blend of vanilla and Earl Grey tea, aptly named the Margate fog. Goodness me, you can even order a beer beside the leadlight windows. It's well worth stepping into church to cap off your Sunday. ●

Words by Alice Hansen

BLACK STAYMAN

BRABANT BELLEFFLEUR

BESS POOL

AL FRISTON

BEDFORDSHIRE FOUNDLING

BELLE PONT DECHAISSE

The Peninsula Experience, Dover

They call it the Far South. And it's pretty accurate. If you continue along the road, you'll reach Cockle Creek, the furthest south you can drive in Australia. So if you're heading this way, you're not on your way to somewhere else, you're on your way to relaxing. And at The Peninsula Experience, you can do just this.

It's rare to have an entire peninsula to yourself but at Esperance Point, these 250 acres are all yours. The property commands 360-degree views across the D'Entrecasteaux Channel, including Bruny Island to the east, the Huon River, and the sometimes snow-capped mountains of the Hartz range.

The accommodation – a turn-of-the-century converted farmhouse combined with modern luxury – takes in full views of Port Esperance Bay and beyond. With room for up to six in three king-sized bedrooms and a spacious deck for outdoor dining, it's easy to slip into "Dover time" out here.

So what is there to do when you're not lost in deep hot tub relaxation on the front deck? You can explore on foot – hidden coves and pebbled waters dotted amongst your own private walking track network. At dusk, meet possums, wallabies and wombats that call the Peninsula home. Don't forget to look up, the stars are something else. You can take the Esperance Coast Road where you'll discover a daffodil farm, Huon Aquaculture salmon farms as well as the windswept and often wild Roaring Beach.

Less than an hour away is the Tahune Airwalk – allowing you to stand nearly 50 metres above the forest floor and walk among the treetops. You'll also find Hastings Caves and Thermal Springs down this way, where chambers, glow worms and flowstone floors await. The pool sits at a pleasant 28 degrees Celsius and there's a lovely rainforest walk where you might come across the resident platypus.

For fishing enthusiasts, it's hard not to get a feed of flathead or squid (calamari) down this way. Cast a line off the boat ramp or one of the sandy beaches and more than likely you'll end up with some fresh fish for dinner.

The Peninsula offers over four kilometres of walking tracks including a woodland walk to views over Lousy Bay where you'll see the salmon farms before descending into heath fields and wetlands. Seal Rocks is a popular 40-minute walk through tall dense forest that will lead you to lichen-covered rocks and the vast Southern Ocean. Alternatively, the Blue Rope Track will take you to Wrack Cove where on a sunny-day a snorkel is a must! ●

peninsulatas.com

Tides Reach, Dover

At Tides Reach, well, you can nearly reach out and touch the still water from the front deck. It's absolute water frontage at Port Esperance Bay. A little over an hour from Hobart, when your toes are sinking into the white sands of Pottery Beach you'll feel far removed from city life.

The cottage lends itself beautifully to those seeking some time away together. Let the calm and serene magic of the water soothe away the day to day stress, sit on the beach and watch as the sun sinks down behind the islands of Faith, Hope and Charity.

Dover is home to many fishing families, so take advantage of the local catch. Pick up some Tassie wine and check what's been hauled in from the clear southern waters – crayfish, abalone, Atlantic salmon, mussels or scallops perhaps? You can also take a few steps off your deck down to the water and cast your own line to see what nibbles. ●

tidesreach.com.au

HUON VALLEY

Red Velvet Lounge

Back in 2003 my wife Cate and I were driving in the depths of winter from the D'Entrecasteaux Channel toward Cygnet, which was in the clutches of an impenetrable pea-soupy fog, and our bellies were grumbling for some lunch. Like a beacon, the warm glow from the Red Velvet Lounge café loomed large in the grey landscape of the street.

HUON VALLEY

The promise of sustenance on such a cold day lured us in and after a warm welcome, a bowl of chunky vegetable soup and a coffee, we ambled around the town surprised and delighted by the friendly greetings we encountered in the shops.

Perhaps it was the feeling of being satiated and warm but the dull streetscape seemed to have morphed into a gilt-edged main drag, golden in the low afternoon sun. We both decided right there and then, this town would be a gorgeous place to live and the Red Velvet Lounge would be a fabulous business to own.

Fast forward six years and I realised a career ambition as a chef to own a business, and as destiny would have it I became the owner of the Red Velvet Lounge. The challenge of fulfilling the huge and as yet untapped potential of the café was my primary motivation for taking the plunge but self-belief, solid experience and great support from friends and family were ballast to steady my journey.

After being at the helm of several businesses throughout my career I had a very firm idea of what I wanted my business to demonstrate and reflect.

I wanted to create a unique and inviting space for everyone in the region and beyond to enjoy, and at the same time foster a culture of excellence. I wanted the best from my staff and suppliers, to support their abilities, and I would lead by example to achieve this.

There have been many inspiring moments that I have experienced as the owner of the Red Velvet Lounge.

A recent example comes to mind. A young couple, new to Cygnet, came to our Tuesday Night Social, a free event during the winter months where we provide sustenance and friendship through hearty soup and fresh baked bread. They were so taken with the Tuesday Night Social idea, the ambience of the café and its food that they bought a house in Cygnet, got married at the Red Velvet Lounge and have since become firm friends of ours.

This is but one instance of the realisation of potential and sense of community I love about the Red Velvet Lounge.

My business is not just a collection of spreadsheets, rather it is about people, customers, staff and suppliers all fostering a sense of belonging and a tangible connection to community. ●

theredvelvetlounge.com.au

RED VELVET LOUNGE

24 Mary Street, Cygnet
theredvelvetlounge.com.au

Red Velvet Lounge is nestled along the main road of peaceful Cygnet – the perfect lunch getaway from central Hobart (45 minutes drive or so). Open seven days with breakfast served until noon, there's no rushing in this cruisy country town. The dinner menus reflect the Huon and Channel area's incredible bounty of produce and it's a chance for Red Velvet (as they say) to frock-up and pretend they're a real grown-up restaurant. They'll make your evening a special one with a unique taste of southern Tasmania. The daytime menu changes with the seasons and is often supplemented by a changing blackboard specials menu that highlights local produce that is available that morning.

CYGNETURE

20 Mary Street, Cygnet
Phone 0408 970 440
cygneture.com.au

Cygneture creates award-winning handcrafted chocolates and confectionery using Tasmania's finest ingredients, focusing on produce from Cygnet, the Huon Valley and Channel. Cygneture products are freshly made and seasonally based, creating an exciting, ever-changing range which includes moulded chocolates, pralines, truffles, honeycomb, chocolate bars and much more, using fruits, nuts, honey, teas, wines and liqueurs sourced directly from their local producers and farmers. The beautiful shop is located at the heritage-listed Old Bank in Cygnet.

THE APPLE SHED – MUSEUM & CIDERHOUSE

2064 Huon Highway, Grove
williesmiths.com.au

In the rustic surrounds of an original apple shed built in 1942, learn about the Huon's fascinating apple heritage told through the eyes of Willie Smith. A range of delicious ciders is available at the cellar door and the café serves a simple menu of the finest regional products. The Apple Shed believes the best tasting food is local, seasonal and sustainable. They work with passionate farmers who, like them, understand that good things take time and great tasting products come from using great quality ingredients. You'll also find a small providore where local producers showcase their products and produce.

HUON VALLEY

MASAAKI SUSHI
Geeveston

Masaaki Sushi specialises in fresh gourmet sushi presented delicately and uniquely. In the small town of Geeveston, Masaaki produces exquisite fresh sushi and revitalising miso soup using local seasonal produce such as Atlantic Salmon, sea urchin roe, Stripey Trumpeter, local vegetables and the pièce de résistance, fresh Tasmanian wasabi.

Masaaki's is open two days a week (Friday and Saturday at time of publication). All sushi is made with love and a big smile by Masaaki Koyama. The café is small so it is highly recommended to book or at least call ahead. You can also catch him rolling *temaki* at the Hobart Farm Gate Market. Follow Masaaki's on Facebook or phone 0408 712 340.

THE KERMANDIE
4518 Main Road, Port Huon
kermandie.com.au

Nestled in Tasmania's beautiful Huon Valley, The Kermandie is just a 45-minute picturesque drive from Hobart. Regardless of the season, The Kermandie is the heart of your southern Tasmania experience. Explore the Huon River, nearby Hastings Caves, Tahune AirWalk, Hartz Mountains National Park and Ida Bay Railway. The Kermandie was built in 1932 to welcome weary travellers to the lower Huon and Esperance district and as a watering hole for timber, orchard and river workers. The Kermandie has been recently refurbished to provide a destination for fine dining and four star accommodation. And you can arrive by road or river.

FRANK'S CIDER BAR AND CAFÉ
frankscider.com.au
3328 Huon Highway, Franklin

Frank's Cider Bar and Cafe is located in the historic town of Franklin (5 minutes south of Huonville). It is part of the Tasmanian Cider Trail, and open seven days a week. The 1870s former St Johns Church Hall is now a cosy café which serves local gourmet produce and offers free cider tasting. Wander through the adjoining Jane Franklin Memorial Museum and Gallery, while you sip a cider and discover the fascinating history of the Huon Valley.

Frank's Cider: Real story ... Real Cider.

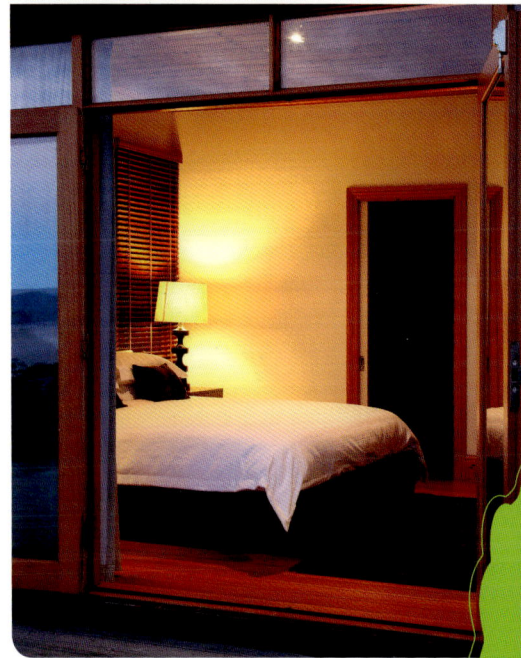

HUON VALLEY

THE BEACH HOUSE, DOVER
driftwoodcottages.com.au

Looking for a peaceful haven to escape to? Exclusively yours, this lovingly-renovated two-bedroom cottage has water and mountain views spilling across the verandah and picture windows. Sunken into the deck you'll find your own private Jacuzzi – a pretty special place from which to peek up at the stars with a Tasmanian pinot in hand. The Beach House is the type of place you'd picture when it's time to escape the busy days – curl up beside the cosy wood fire or take a stroll along the waterside walking tracks just out the front door. The Beach House is one of a range of Driftwood Cottages on offer in the Far South region at the base of the Huon Valley.

TIDES REACH, DOVER
tidesreach.com.au

At Tides Reach, well, you can nearly reach out and touch the still water from the front deck. It's absolute water frontage at Port Esperance Bay. A little over an hour from Hobart, when your toes are sinking into the white sands of Pottery Beach you'll feel far removed from city life.

The cottage lends itself beautifully to those seeking some time away together. Let the calm and serene magic of the water soothe away the day to day stress, sit on the beach and watch as the sun sinks down behind the islands of Faith, Hope and Charity.

Dover is home to many fishing families, so take advantage of the local catch. Pick up some Tassie wine and check what's been hauled in from the clear southern waters – crayfish, abalone, Atlantic salmon, mussels or scallops perhaps? You can also take a few steps off your deck down to the water and cast your own line to see what nibbles.

THE PENINSULA
peninsulatas.com

A little piece of paradise, nestled in the beauty and tranquility of Tasmania's Huon Valley. The Peninsula Experience provides the ultimate luxury getaway. With exclusivity, panoramic water views and your own private hot tub under the stars this unique property offers unsurpassed accommodation with 250 acres of wilderness, water and wildlife to explore. The Peninsula offers a beautiful mix of worlds – this stunning turn-of-the-century farmhouse is situated to take full advantage of expansive water views from every aspect. Perfect for a romantic escape or an intimate adult retreat, with three luxurious king bedrooms, two bathrooms and contemporary décor.

Coal River Valley
+ Richmond

Richmond and its riches

"That used to be mine," came a voice from over the road. I didn't know someone was watching me photograph their rubbish, and the Richmond local seemed amused enough to peer over her newspaper.

"I decided it was time to get rid of it. It's quite old," she carried on with a smile. She wore a patterned summer dress and was taking a moment to enjoy the afternoon sunshine.

She was right. There are plenty of things that are "a bit old" here in Richmond. But unlike her television set, these are not the type of things to be left on the curb. Old is new again here in Richmond. And gosh they're doing it well.

The locals here enjoy a steadier pace in life and it doesn't hurt to join them for a day. A good way to do so is to equip yourself with two wooden oars. There's a certain old-fashioned charm that comes with rowing someone upstream. And if you're slower than the family of baby ducklings bobbing beside you, you're on track to becoming a local.

Us Tasmanians can likely all say we've seen the Richmond Bridge, but have you seen its underbelly? Floating in the shadow of convict-laid bricks is a special way to see Australia's oldest bridge. Swapping seats in a tiny wooden boat to capture it on camera is less wise. But that's another story.

For those who prefer dry land, the Richmond Boathouse offers more than just rowboats. They have two-wheeled transport and gourmet picnics too –

including one offering that brims with fresh Tassie berries. It's the perfect reason to find a shady patch of grass to park on.

Wander the town, step inside the maze, swing a golf club, visit a Tassie devil, sip a pinot, stock up on old-fashioned lollies. A trip down the Coal River Valley to Richmond is an experience that will take you back. That will slow you down. Even the bathroom at a local vineyard invites you to stay a while!

Wind your way round a few more bends and you'll find another cheery local. Who wouldn't be smiling if they looked out over a giant strawberry patch? When asked if I should pay my $3 now for the punnet we were about to pick ourselves she began to laugh.

"I'm not going to chase you down the road," she said smiling behind her sunglasses. "And make sure you try

some as you go, won't you?" With that, she stepped back into her makeshift office and sat down to the paper.

Another lesson learnt. Honesty is a given in these parts, it's important not to hurry and savouring the experience is a must. We did just that. Next stop, a favourite, Puddleduck Vineyard.

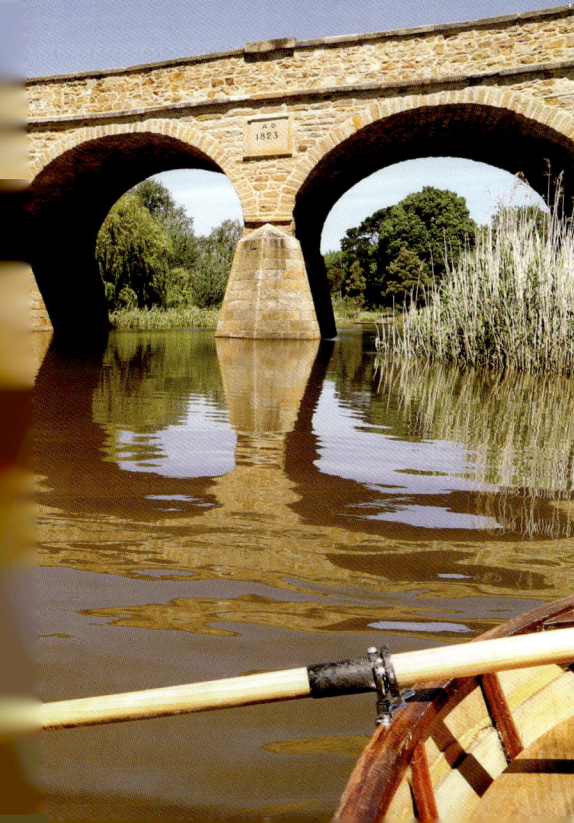

What the locals

What the locals love

TIPS FROM THOSE WHO LIVE HERE

Coal River Valley & Richmond

> Puddleduck Vineyard – award-winning wine delivered with family warmth and the only place where reverse-BYO is encouraged. Take your picnic and they'll supply a delicious drop!

> Pretty as a picture, Richmond Bridge is Australia's oldest bridge still in use today. And the best way to appreciate it during summer is floating beneath the arches in a wooden row boat. Richmond Park Boathouse also offers bike hire and gourmet picnic hampers to enjoy on the green for those who want to make an afternoon of it.

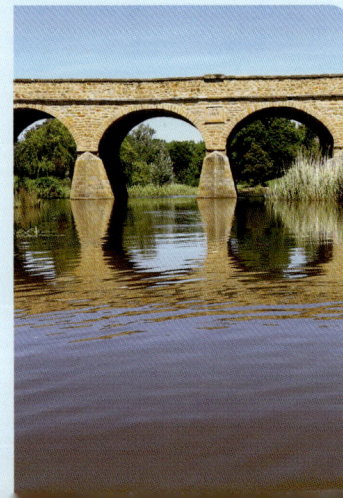

There's a quick hello to the "wine corgi" and of course the owners Darren and Jackie. This is a place where reverse-BYO is quite the trend. They supply the Bubbleduck bubbles or award-winning pinot for instance, and you bring your own tasty treats to enjoy by the lake.

A quick wander through the vines at Frogmore Vineyard, and a late afternoon drink, then it's time to head back to Hobart. But not without hopping on the children's play equipment first.

No, it's probably not allowed, but it's a fitting way to end a day in the Coal River Valley. Start the day rushed, ease into a local's pace and by the end of the day you too might find yourself perched on a bobbing barrel. Not because you planned to, but because when the day slows you can see it as a child might. Abandon replaces restraint – and you're in the moment. Hell, at least kick off your shoes and feel the grass beneath your toes! The city can wait. ●

PUDDLEDUCK VINEYARD
992 Richmond Road, Richmond
puddleduckvineyard.com.au

Puddleduck Vineyard is owned and operated by Darren and Jackie Brown, and offers a fun and quirky wine tasting experience that is sure to make you feel right at home – usually accompanied by a pat of their pet duck Lucky or wine dog Polly! Puddleduck is a Reverse BYO®, meaning that you bring the food to have with their wines and ciders (beer and soft drinks/tea and coffee). If you prefer you can take advantage of a Tasmanian cheese platter or just taste at the bar. Puddleduck is also home to Lost Pippin Cider, so you can taste those as well!

POOLEY WINES
1431 Richmond Road, Richmond
pooleywines.com.au

Producer of premium Tasmanian cool-climate wines, Pooley Wines is a small, family-owned winery producing premium Tasmanian wines from two vineyards in the Coal River Valley. The late Denis and Margaret Pooley planted the family's first vines in 1985. Today, the business is managed by their son, John Pooley, supported by his son, viticulturalist Matthew Pooley and daughter, winemaker Anna Pooley.

Their cellar door is located in old converted stables at the rear of their 1830s Georgian home at the heritage-listed Belmont property overlooking historic Richmond.

Each year, they carefully hand pick our grapes and take them to our small winery to be crushed on the same day. Small batch winemaking allows them to treat each parcel of fruit differently, allowing for true expressions of terroir.

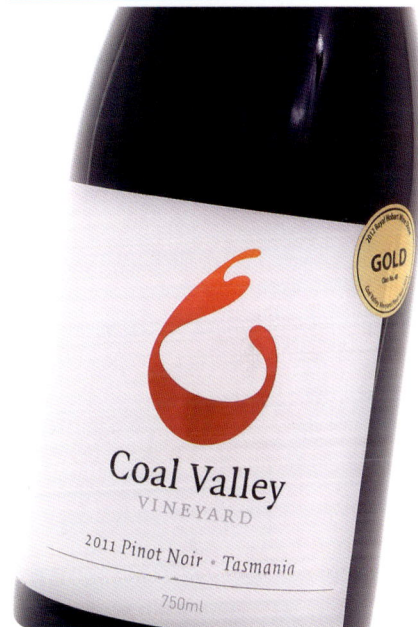

COAL VALLEY VINEYARD
257 Richmond Road, Richmond
coalvalley.com.au

Dining with Coal Valley Vineyard wine: a family winery passionate about making (small quantities) of great wine. Start with their sparkling. It has "the loveliest mousse of silky-soft minuscule bubbles anyone could hope for" (Tom Stevenson, the world authority on Champagne). Their delightfully crisp dry citrus riesling complements the best Tassie oysters and Spring Bay scallops; Rannoch quail is a delicious match for their golden chardonnay. A rack of lamb and a bottle of Coal Valley Vineyard Pinot Noir and you could stop right there ... or you could just squeeze in some of the island's fabulous cheeses with the TGR (a hint of sweet) riesling.

Channel + Bruny Island

What the locals love

TIPS FROM THOSE WHO LIVE HERE
Channel + Bruny Island

CHANNEL + BRUNY ISLAND

> You'll find Coningham Beach about half an hour south of Hobart. Dotted with boatsheds and boasting a sandstone headland to explore, this quiet beach is the definition of peaceful.

> Meet the "ladies" at Grandvewe Cheeses in Woodbridge – the cutest sheep – especially those who have moved onto the "retirement village".

> There's a small town by the name of Snug. It's cute. And the walk to Snug Falls is well worth the wander.

> Look for a rock arch on Bruny Island – you'll find it along the Cape Queen Elizabeth Walk when you reach the beach. It's pretty special.

> Albino wallabies? Head to Bruny and you might just meet one!

127

CHANNEL + BRUNY ISLAND

Satellite Island – your own private island

Satellite Island is a privately-owned island in the beautiful D'Entrecasteaux Channel on the south-east coast of Tasmania, not far from Bruny Island.

The island is surrounded by sheer sea cliffs, sunny coves and pebble beaches and encircled by an ancient rock shelf brimming with wild shellfish. Shuck oysters straight from the rock shelf, fish for crayfish, abalone and scallops, light a fire on the pebble beach at Sunset Bay and watch the sun set across the Southern Ocean. Kayak, take one of the beautiful walks around the Island or simply relax on the Summer House deck or at the Boathouse and take in the surrounding Tasmanian wilderness. Explore nearby Bruny Island and sample the fabulous local produce, walks and adventure tours. Satellite Island is a unique destination and yours alone to explore.

Visit satelliteisland.com.au to find out more.

Bruny Island Long Weekend

"It would be vain of me to attempt to describe my feelings when I beheld this lonely harbour lying at the world's end, separated as it were from the rest of the universe – 'twas nature and nature in her wildest mood ..." Admiral Bruni D'Entrecasteaux

We make our way down this very same channel, appropriately named the D'Entrecasteaux Channel, similarly in awe of this wild, raw and ruggedly beautiful part of the world. The only difference?

We are aboard a high-speed catamaran with latte in hand.

As we set foot on Bruny Island, bags are quickly whisked from our hands by guides Alex and Rob and bundled into the waiting van. These two effortlessly take care of everything; there'll be no pack to carry on this trip.

We exchange excited glances as Rob Knight, the creator and owner of The Bruny Island Long Weekend, drives us to the starting point of our first walking expedition. Today we're traversing 12 kilometres to enjoy lunch atop Cape Queen Elizabeth. The sandy track opens out before us, inviting us to explore the natural beauty of this island the superior way, on foot.

As the cheery chatter echoes down the line of walkers getting to know each other, we are greeted with our first local. A shiny black tiger snake stretches out across the track, absorbing the rays of our sunny morning. As I run with saucer-wide eyes back through the group, I realise I'm the only one less than willing to greet our new mate. The others are delighted.

We walk on through coastal heathland followed by a steady climb up Mars Bluff. From here we are rewarded with a gorgeous view of The Neck that joins north and south Bruny. But what lies ahead is equally special. Down below beckons remote Miles Beach. It's glorious, untouched and entirely devoid of human life.

The pace quickens as we head down the dunes, eager to set foot on the squeaky white sands and watch the turquoise waves tumble in. On this breathless day, the sound is exquisite as salty water quietly meets its sandy curve.

We climb up through eucalypt forest, enjoying the sweet sounds of endemic birds, carefully crossing mutton bird rookeries before reaching our lunch pinnacle. Over a delicious walnut, feta and spinach salad teamed with a pumpkin and feta quiche we soak up views across Adventure Bay and beyond, as the striking Hound's Tooth rock formation rises up from the water behind us.

With full tummies, we venture back down to Miles Beach, unlace our boots and splash our way ankle-deep back along to some fascinating fossils, a Jurassic dolerite rock arch and some impressive beach caves. Alex's encyclopaedic knowledge continues to impress, from fossils, to birdlife, to explorers to practically any leaf we brush past.

Gourmet treats

After our lengthy walk, Rob deems it necessary to reward us. After a quick reverse down a dusty dirt road, we arrive at the Bruny Island Marine Farm. Alex is quick to pour a refreshing elderflower with sparkling water and ice to quench our thirst, as former stockbroker Sam leisurely cruises up to his farm aboard his oyster boat and casually shucks us a few plump oysters.

Our Sydney-sider squeals with delight as she accepts a freshly opened oyster straight from the farmer's hand, standing ankle-deep in the salty waters they reside in. It is then on to the Bruny Island Cheese Company to enjoy a delicious cheese tasting. We tuck two of our favourites away for later.

Next stop: our luxury camp. Well-secluded on 100 acres of land boasting ample wildlife, with towering blackwoods, dogwoods, and tall stringybarks, this little haven represents the perfect place to retreat. We each are shown to our finely-appointed tents then the race is on for first shower. With the flip of a table tennis paddle atop a stick (red means engaged) we have our very own outdoor

forest shower. Three modest walls hide us from the rest of the camp while an open-air window lets us breathe in bush air and watch the birds weave between the treetops. It's so invigorating we could be forgiven for forgetting our stark state!

Night is when the Bruny Island Long Weekend guides really turn up the gourmet heat. On arrival in the "dining house" we're met with vibrant orange honey-suckle flowers on a long rustic table. With a celebratory giggle, the first guest opts for bubbles and we promptly all follow suit. In moments we are each handed a Tasmanian Jansz on the deck under the setting sun. As we discuss how wonderful life is, Alex and Rob busy themselves in preparing us fresh Bruny Island oysters, Woodbridge Smokehouse cold-smoked trout, delicious dips and wood-fired bread.

The menu for the evening better resembles that of a fine-dining restaurant than a camp-kitchen. Bruny Island wallaby carpaccio with radishini and Grandvewe pecorino is followed by Spring Bay mussels in delicious saffron cream and perfectly-cooked Murrayfield lamb from northern Bruny served with lemon, garlic and thyme.

Wild and windy

Day two begins as light fills the tent and a few happy chirps ring through the valley. I lie there and absorb the sound of leaves colliding in the morning breeze. Today we are bound for South Bruny National Park, and as if on cue the wind picks up and gives this desolate corner of the island an even more rugged personality.

The first 45 minutes of the walk takes in the length of Cloudy Bay Beach. It's windswept and wild, leading us into coastal heath and a steady climb to the headland for views across the Friars Rocks. Settling in for lunch, it's a captivating feeling to look across the Southern Ocean, knowing that 2500km beyond lies Antarctica. Breathtaking views out to Cape Bruny Lighthouse in the west and the distant Southern Ranges of the Tasmanian mainland complete the panorama.

Following our hard work, we are again subjected to gourmet treats. Next stop is Australia's southern-most vineyard. We know the drill; we get to sample the wares and Rob scoops up an armful for camp.

Later that evening we are spoilt with blue-eye trevalla, toasted hazelnut and rocket salad as well as a perfectly-rested fillet of Cape Grim beef served with pink-eye potatoes, vine ripened tomatoes and steamed greens.

The last day begins with scrambled eggs, crispy bacon and delicious Huon mushrooms. After a short wet-forest walk we hop aboard Rob Pennicott's award-winning wilderness and wildlife adventure cruise to enjoy some of the highest sea cliffs in the southern hemisphere as well as dolphins, bold male seals and cruising albatross.

We then enjoy our final lunch overlooking Adventure Bay before meeting our seaplane pilot. It's a rare site to see a pilot with his trousers rolled up, knee deep in water, and a plane with an anchor attached. Bumping across the waves at speed, it's a thrill as we rise gently above the water. But as the capital sneaks into view once more, it's with a hint of sadness that Bruny Island grows smaller in the distance. What a long weekend – the perfect blend of walking, adventure, luxury and laughter. ●

brunyislandlongweekend.com.au

Words and images by Alice Hansen
First appeared in Great Walks Magazine

HERBACEOUS TOURS

Any of us can head across to Bruny or drive down the Channel and enjoy a day feasting on Tasmania's finest produce, but when you go with Sally, you have a completely different experience. The day I hopped aboard Herbaceous Tours, I was directed through farm gates I'd never pushed open (despite being a local myself), met makers and sampled cheese from their knife, tasted produce right there in the paddock, and watched as abalone was prepared before my eyes. Here's what to expect on one of Sally's tours. From Hobart to Richmond, she takes you off the beaten tourist trail, and will even tailor tours just for you.

Huon/Channel Tour

Saffron, cider, wine, apples and honey anyone?

This part of Tasmania was once the world's largest producer of apples. The region still produces a mighty fine crisp apple, but today there's plenty more produce on offer.

As many of the tour destinations are working farms, Sally's tours change slightly depending on the season and availability of farmers and producers on the day. On a Huon/Channel adventure, guests can look forward to hitting at least four of the following: Will Smith Apple Shed, Tasmanian Saffron Farm, Panorama Vineyard, Nutpatch, Grandvewe Sheep Cheesery, Van Diemen Native Peppers, Hartzview Vineyard, Home Hill Winery, Kelty Farm (organic black angus, heritage pigs and organic apples) and Miellerie Honey. Lunch is usually at the Red Velvet Lounge in Cygnet where Steve (the chef) uses local products. Steve won Country Style magazine's Regional Chef of the Year Award (Australia wide) so you are guaranteed a great experience.

The producers you will meet on any of Sally's tours are very passionate about what they do and what they produce and are keen to share their knowledge and stories. For example, what do you know about saffron? Nicky and Terry Noonan were the first saffron growers in Tasmania, and while you enjoy a homemade morning tea Terry will guide you through the growing process, explain what makes Tasmanian saffron the highest grade in the world, show you some samples from around the world and let you into the secrets of the amazing medical benefits of saffron – and that's just one stop! ●

herbaceoustours.com.au

The Fox Hole and Huon Pine Picnic Planks

Some Tasmanians just have a way of carving out a special career path. And this is certainly so for husband and wife team, Lizz and Gilbert. For the past 16 years the couple have lived in the sleepy town of Woodbridge, down the Channel where summer time involves "jetty jumping", playing around with boats and diving for abalone.

Lizz is a pastry chef who runs a small gourmet food business with her family, operating from Woodbridge and Gilbert loves rare species of timber. The Huon pine picnic plank is Gilbert's much-loved creation, a favourite at Salamanca Market for those on the hunt for a memorable engagement gift or simply a piece of ancient beauty to place their Bruny Island cheese upon.

Meet these two and all you'll see are smiles. They're both mad about food. They both love markets and festivals. And they both love to chat. Gilbert will tell you about Tasmanian history and the local surrounds, while Lizz will happily invite you to stay in the Fox Hole, a quaint one-bedroom cottage the couple have created out the back of their home.

It doesn't get any more authentic or more Tasmanian than spending a little time in Woodbridge at the Fox Hole. Book in at the charming self-contained studio and you'll have your very own fruit orchard and free roaming chooks out your back door. Pick some apples or mulberries in season, or help yourself to a lime or lemon for your gin and tonic.

From Woodbridge you can easily hop across to Bruny Island, explore the Huon Valley or stop by Grandvewe Cheesery where the sheep are fondly known as "the girls". This peaceful part of the world is brimming with fresh produce, roadside stalls and friendly locals. ●

Salamanca Market: stall 221
huonpinepicnicplanks.com.au

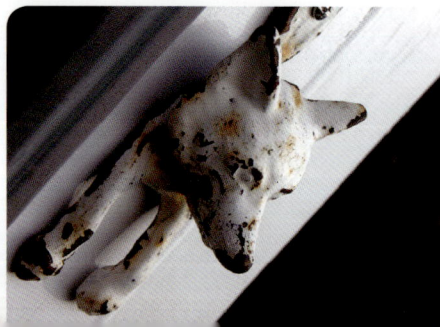

Bruny Island Cheese Company – *passion, seduction and cheese*

We chatted ... would you believe ... over cheese. As Nick Haddow raises another piece off the wooden board, his words are simple: "I love cheese."

His comment isn't designed to convince me, nor is it said with much conscious attention. Yet, its quiet passion is unmistakable. Nick really does love cheese. I figured that out when I pushed him to single out a favourite – it was like choosing between his own two children.

"It began with a bucket of goats milk in the Barossa Valley," says Nick, "when some friends and I were running a restaurant and no one knew how to make cheese. I thought I'd give it a go. From that day I was fascinated – by the tradition, challenge and seduction of cheese making."

Yes, that's right. According to Nick, the process of cheese making is "incredibly beautiful and sensual". It's scientific as well as creative, and it is the confluence of both that seduced Nick. His love of cheese making took him from the Barossa to fine restaurants in Sydney and Melbourne, to the UK, across to Japan where he fell in love with his now wife, and from Japan straight to Pyengana.

"Now that was a change of scenery. Japan to Pyengana. We had no idea what we were letting ourselves in for," Nick explains. "It was the middle of nowhere, even by Tasmanian standards. But it was such a privilege to be part of the Pyengana cheese making story."

Nick learnt much during his time in this rural patch of Tassie, not least of all that he could do it for himself. Working seven days a week and 15 hours a day, Nick and wife Leonie took a weekend off from Pyengana and ended up on Bruny Island. The love affair was about as instant as Nick falling for his cheese. In a short time they'd bought a house on Bruny and were making cheese at what he describes as a micro-level.

Eleven years on, Nick's cellar door on Bruny is 20 times the size of its humble beginnings and barely able to contain his cheese enthusiasts. The cheese-loving pilgrims come by ferry, they stay for wood-fired pizza beneath the trees and they watch as cheese matures before their eyes.

Now they can also source cheese in the Salamanca Arts Centre, where tucked under a staircase is a pantry brimming with Tassie produce, and of course plenty of cheese. They come for the likes of Tom, Oen and C2. Tom, incidentally likes to be rubbed, and Nick's raw milk creation, C2, is the cheese he's most proud of. Owen, he insists, "can be very exciting".

Despite some non-practicalities of choosing Bruny as home for his cheese making, Nick doesn't regret it for a moment. He loves the challenge and the lifestyle. When he's not wearing his white gumboots that feature in the logo, you might find him walking with his family out to one of his favourite Bruny beaches along the Cape Queen Elizabeth walking track.

And while the trials and expense of establishing on the island sound staggering, he goes and tells me he's about to open a micro brewery. We can only hope that Nick is equally seduced by his Bruny brews. ●

eat & drink

eat, stay & play

eat & drink

GET SHUCKED

1735 Bruny Island Main Road
brunyislandoysters.com

Get Shucked began in 2004 when lease 204 in Great Bay was purchased by Bruny Island resident Joe Bennett. The lease was one the original oyster farms on Bruny Island back in the 70s. Get Shucked produces Pacific oysters year round and supply some of Australia's top restaurants. In 2013 Joe and partner Nicole opened a fully-licensed oyster bar overlooking the farm, where you can see all the live harvesting, grading and your oysters being shucked. Natural, Kilpatrick, panko crumbed, steamed oriental, oyster paté and more. There is also a range of local sparkling, beer, wine and cider.

BRUNY ISLAND LONG WEEKEND

brunyislandlongweekend.com.au

The Bruny Island Long Weekend is a luxury three-day guided food, wine and walking tour featuring spectacular coastal scenery, wildlife and amazing food. When you book during December, just mention Tailored Tasmania to receive a complimentary copy of Bruny Island – Food from the Edge of the World by Richard Bennett and Jill Mure. It'll be mailed free to anywhere in Australia, inspiring you prior to your Bruny adventure. On the trip, you'll harvest local oysters, spot nocturnal wildlife, visit a cheese producer and venture into the Southern Ocean to spot dolphins, whales and fur seals. Accommodation is in a luxurious forest camp, with dinner prepared as you enjoy wine round a roaring camp fire. You'll depart by catamaran from Hobart and return by seaplane.

HARTZVIEW WINE CENTRE

70 Dillons Road, Gardners Bay
hartzview.com.au
(03) 6295 1623

All-day lunches served in a café with magnificent views. Tastings from hand-picked pinot noir, rosé, sauvignon blanc, chardonnays and a large range of preservative-free fruit ports and liqueurs, including Tasmanian cassis and mead. Linger and enjoy a combined vineyard and cheese platter, Devonshire tea or a specialty dessert and great coffee. Take a stroll into history on the self-guided heritage pickers hut walk. Nestled behind the hedge is a peaceful, self-contained warm spa cottage where you can enjoy a few days unwinding and relaxation, or base yourself for touring the Huon/Channel/Bruny Island region.

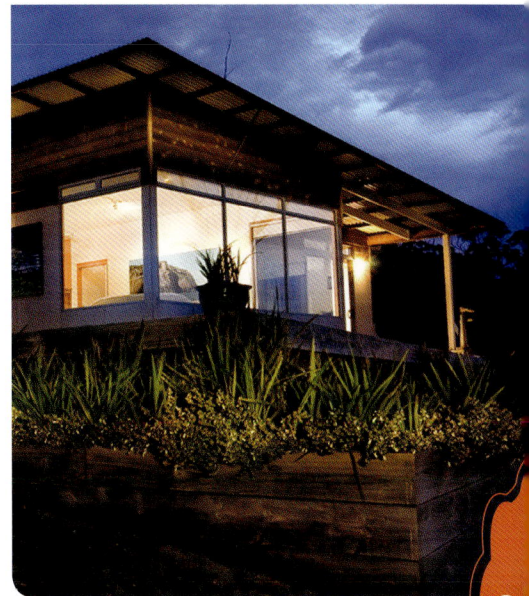

ADVENTURE BAY RETREAT
Bruny Island
adventurebayretreat.com.au

At Adventure Bay Retreat you can choose between two premium boutique accommodation options – The Lodge or The Cottage. The three-bedroom lodge accommodates up to eight people and The Cottage is the perfect couple's romantic weekend retreat. Nestled into the open bushland of Adventure Bay on 33 acres you are guaranteed privacy. Surrounded by wallabies including the white wallaby (unique to the area), great photographic opportunities exist while experiencing the local wildlife close to the beautiful white sands of Adventure Bay Beach.

WOODBRIDGE HILL HIDEAWAY
369 Woodbridge Hill Road, Woodbridge
woodbridgehillhideaway.com.au

This is one beautiful little getaway. Get 10 per cent off, or 20 per cent off if you stay three nights or more, at this magic hideaway when you mention Tailored Tasmania. This luxurious holiday retreat near Hobart is nestled into some of the highest parts of Woodbridge Hill, just 20-minutes drive south of Hobart. The commanding views of Bruny Island and the D'Entrecasteaux Channel all the way to the Tasman Peninsula perfectly enhance the private studio apartment. This retreat brims with tasteful and indulgent features. The windows by glass-artist Ruth Downham, the heated slate bathroom floors, reclining leather couches, indoor swimming pool, salvaged Tasmanian blackheart sassafras timbers and spas are just some of the modern, stylish features.

CHEZ DISCOVERY
Bruny Island
brunyislandexperience.com

Labillardiere Estate and Chez Discovery "house of discovery" is not just a place to stay – whirlwind paces drop to zephyr breezes and stresses pale in this place of unrivalled privacy. Magical views across Great Taylors Bay to the mountain ranges of southern Tasmania, with flora, fauna, long walking tracks, private beaches, wetlands, art, folly and a quiet that we forget exists are waiting. Book an "Aquila" Sealegs adventure if you feel like an amphibious boat trip – they'll drive you from the front door straight into the bay. Chez Discovery is a great base for exploring or for writing your memoirs, so go on, give yourself that break you deserve and discover art, discover nature and discover self!

CLOUDY BAY BEACH HOUSE

Bruny Island
cloudybaybeachhouse.com

Bruny Island's Cloudy Bay Beach House
view is utterly addictive. Simply beautiful
and beautifully simple, this contemporary,
private and relaxed three-bedroom
and three-bathroom residence is fully
equipped for your enjoyment. Twin
pavilions and four decks make the
residence the perfect location to wind
down and revive. Nestled in naturally-
vegetated dunes with spectacular,
panoramic views to iconic Cloudy Bay,
South Bruny National Park, Cape Bruny
and the vast Southern Ocean. As one
guest put it, "I had intended to get some
work done, but instead, I watched clouds
and was completely mesmerised!" With
surprises awaiting, you'll want to linger,
be seduced by ocean breezes, wish upon
the southern stars and stay forever …

Heritage Highway
& HIGHLANDS

TIPS FROM THOSE WHO LIVE HERE

Heritage Highway & Highlands

> In historic Oatlands, look for a fellow with a shop full of treasures. They're well priced and you'll know when you've found him.

> Food tastes so much better in the wild outdoors, doesn't it? Fresh Tassie produce is at its best when shared with good friends. Head to the highlands to find your perfect outdoor dining table.

> Highland trout fishing – once locals are hooked they may not speak for hours – or days.

> Stop in at Kempton and by appointment you can meet the only fellow in the country making 100% rye whiskey, using bio-fuel.

> At Bothwell, swing a hickory club on Australia's oldest golf course.

> Join the custodians of Shene Estate for a unique behind-the-scenes tour of this historic site. A pastoral holding since the first land grant by Governor Lachlan Macquarie in 1819, you can delve into the fascinating past of fortunes and felons in Tasmania.

Ratho Farm

Thanks to the passions of those who set foot on Van Diemens Land in the early days, Tasmania has been gifted with many firsts. We are proud owners of Australia's oldest brewery and oldest pub – clearly they had their priorities in order.

Yet, we rarely boast about being home to the country's oldest golf course – nor the patch of land in Bothwell that happened to be one of the earliest inland settlements – Ratho Farm. For the boatload of early Scots including Alexander Reid though, it wasn't all swinging hickory clubs and sipping whisky in the central highlands. There were bushrangers to contend with, as early settler Jane Williams (nee Reid) recalls vividly.

The others took axes and began to break open the chests of drawers, boxes, etc., when my mother with her usual admirable composure told them it was a pity to destroy the furniture, and if they were determined to help themselves she would open the drawers, and getting her bunch of keys threw everything open, while they turned out the stores of clothing and other comforts my father had provided, thinking to give us all the necessaries of life which could not then be obtained in the bush.

It wouldn't be the only attack at Ratho Farm during those fragile and spirited early days. Ratho Farm played host to colourful characters ranging from Melbourne Cup winners, bushrangers, 100-year-old gardeners, fierce political debates, golfing royalty and one of England's best known artists. These folk became pieces of the Ratho patchwork, each leaving their mark.

Today, the farm buildings built by those early settlers provide an important heritage backdrop to Ratho Farm Golf Links. Several settlers were from families and places quite partial to a game of golf back in Scotland, and were determined

to continue this pastime in Tasmania. So over three generations, the Reid family created the Ratho Farm Golf Links, which are now recognised as one of the world's best-preserved ancient golfing grounds.

Like most early private courses, the first tee and eighteenth green were positioned close to the homestead and outbuildings. From here, the dairy, skin shed, convict cottage and bakery were all in Alexander's full view.

Following a grand restoration headed by Greg Ramsay (fourth generation on the property and is well known for developing Barnhougle Dunes), Ratho Farm is now a tourism destination featuring

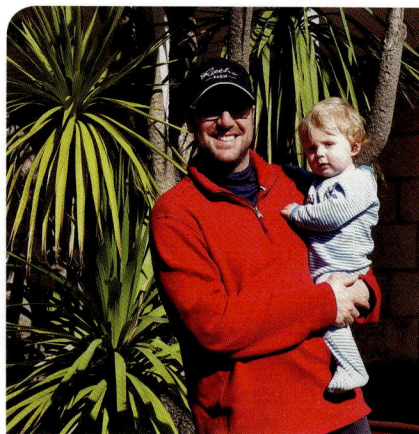

LOCAL RULES.

1. A ball lying in any rabbit scrape, hoof print, or cart rut, or on, or within two feet of any stone, may be lifted and dropped, not nearer the hole, without penalty.

2. A ball lying in any of the small drains at the first hole, or in either of the two small drains nearest to the second green, may be lifted and dropped, not nearer the hole, without penalty.

3. A ball lying in the garden near the third green shall be lifted and dropped clear of the fence, but not nearer the hole, under penalty of one stroke.

4. "Out of Bounds." Any part of the Great Lake Road, and over the fences to the left of seventh and eighth fairways. Penalty, loss of distance.

29/2678 Mercury, Hobart

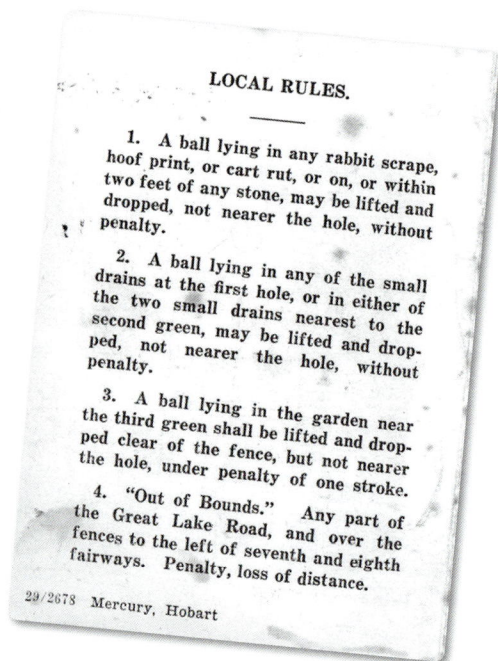

accommodation for up to 40 guests in renovated farm buildings and the original homestead, a golf links with restored and expanded 18 holes and a dynamic heritage interpretation experience. Oh, and Australia's oldest chook house.

As with any farm, all work, rest and play revolves around the Homestead. It's changed enormously since the early settlers were ransacked by bushrangers on the verandah in the early 1800s. It has been restored to its former glory. Visitors can cosy up by the big open fire with a Tasmanian whisky from the Highlands

Bar or explore the History Room and how those three Alexander's shaped Tasmania's central highlands. Visitors can stay in the original homestead, farm barns or convict cottages on the banks of the Clyde River, buildings that whisper a story of Ratho's past.

In keeping with the traditions of Old Scotland, Ratho Farm will remain a public course and is open to all, every day of the week. Hickory clubs are available to enjoy the course as the earliest golfers once did. The newly re-opened course features a unique mix of holes,

including the open and windswept old holes, restored original holes in a parkland setting, and four newly designed holes along the Clyde river bank towards neighbouring Nant Distillery.

Today the golf balls might not be made of kangaroo skin stuffed with merino wool, nor are there bushrangers at the ready to attack, but the history of Ratho Farm is very much alive as the Ramsay family add a new chapter to Ratho's well-documented past. ●

rathofarm.com

BONORONG WILDLIFE SANCTUARY
593 Briggs Road, Brighton
bonorong.com.au

Bonorong Wildlife Sanctuary aims to rescue, rehabilitate and release orphaned and injured native animals to the wild. All funds raised are directed to projects to conserve, rescue, and rehabilitate wildlife including breeding programs to boost declining numbers of the Tasmanian devil and the eastern quoll, coordinating a 24hr wildlife rescue service to cope with the very high number of injured and orphaned wildlife, and running Tasmania's largest seabird rehabilitation facility. The Sanctuary is also planning to build Tasmania's first wildlife veterinary clinic with a vet dedicated to providing care, advice and equipment free of charge to native Tasmanian wildlife and their carers. Visitors have the opportunity to meet species now found only in Tasmania. Join the public tours at 11.30am and 2pm or book a private behind-the-scenes tour.

AUSTRALASIAN GOLF MUSEUM
Market Place, Bothwell
ausgolfmuseum.com

The museum tells the story of how golf evolved from a game played by a handful of villages on Scotland's east coast, to now being a truly international game. The museum illustrates why the early settlers in historic Bothwell became Australia's first golfing community, with the nearby Ratho Farm Golf Links recognised as Australia's oldest golf course. The evolution of the game is explained through the different eras, as defined by the changing golf ball; from Feathery (1400s to mid 1800s) to Gutta-percha (1850s to 1900) to Haskell (turn of the century to World War II) and the modern balls. Many of Tasmania's champion golfers are featured, from Australia's first born champions, the Pearce Brothers, to Lucy Arthur, Len Nettlefold, Elvie Whitesides, the Toogoods and the Goggins. You'll also find the Tasmanian Golf Hall of Fame housed here.

BELGROVE DISTILLERY
3121 Midland Highway, Kempton
belgrovedistillery.com.au

About 45 minutes up the Heritage Highway you'll find Peter Bignell's distillery. It's one of those classic Tassie stories – Peter produced rye as a trusty windbreak and for feeding his stock, now he's producing spicy rye whisky that's found its way to some of Sydney's finest bars. What's more, Peter built his copper pot with his bare hands. It is fired with biodiesel that he makes from waste cooking oil from a roadhouse near his farm. For those who enjoy a spicy note, Peter's 100 per cent rye whisky provides a kick you won't expect. Visits are by appointment only.

Tasman Peninsula

TASMAN PENINSULA

> Where is the only place Abel Tasman set foot? Right here at Bangor. Now you can be treated to freshly-shucked oysters and regional wine at a rustic cellar door Abel could have only dreamed of stumbling across.

> Walking into the huge sand dunes at Crescent Bay on the Tasman Peninsula

> Fish and chips on the wharf at Dunalley – so good!

> Head to Remarkable Cave and watch the local surfers followed by a ghost tour at Port Arthur.

> Head to Plunket Point for a picnic – about five minutes walk from the Coal Mines Historic Site at Saltwater River. It's a beautiful spot to eat with a phenomenal outlook and lots of ruins and peace. Nearby is also a great walk from Lime Bay to Lagoon Beach – it never disappoints.

> For those who like a camping or caravanning adventure, White Beach Caravan Park is a popular destination for Hobart families. The local jetty at White Beach is great for squidding; who doesn't like fresh calamari for dins?

GILLESPIE'S GINGER BEER
Salamanca Market
gillespiesgingerbeer.com.au

Gillespie's Ginger Beer is made using traditional brewing methods from a recipe that is over 100 years old – perhaps that's why it's so delicious. The iconic Tasmanian drink is available in both alcoholic and non-alcoholic varieties and is entirely preservative and additive free. Using only the finest ingredients including natural rainwater, Tasmanian native pepper berries and organic ginger, Gillespie's is a premium sip. Proudly brewed on the east coast of Tasmania in a family-run business, Gillespie's can be found at specially shops, cafés and restaurants as well as Salamanca Market every Saturday.

WILLIAM MCHENRY & SONS DISTILLERY
229 Radnor Road, Port Arthur
mchenrydistillery.com.au

The McHenry Distillery is the southern-most whisky distillery in Australia. Located at Port Arthur its southern location takes advantage of the cool, moist maritime environment which provides the perfect conditions for whisky making. The Distillery uses its own abundant clear spring water, which flows off Mount Arthur and directly into the distillery, and becomes the heart of the developing spirit. They specialise in hand-made single malt Tasmanian whisky and other high-quality spirits like London Dry Gin, Sloe Gin, Navy Strength Gin, Barrel Aged Gin and Vodka and take pride in their range of products.

REDBANKS
276 Masons Road, Nugent
redbankstas.com.au

Redbanks is an adventure playground situated in the south-east where many sports and activities can be enjoyed. Archery, slingshot, rifle and clay-target shooting, fly and lure fishing, kayaking, mountain bike riding as well as team sports like volleyball, soccer, cricket and football can all be enjoyed. They now have a purpose-built 8 kilometre mud and obstacle course with over 40 different and challenging obstacles. Their fully-licensed lodge caters for groups of up to 120 people. Any function can be catered for, ranging from bucks and hens parties, birthday and family groups, weddings, through to conference and business groups for up to 300 people. Their airstrip allows for scenic flights or to arrive in style for a day's fun.

TASMAN PENINSULA

147

Bangor Wine & Oyster Shed

It doesn't get much better than eating freshly-shucked oysters overlooking the bay where they are grown and drinking a glass of wine beside the vines on which the grapes ripened. At Bangor Wine & Oyster Shed this is what's in store, along with a glimpse into Tasmanian farming life.

Located just 500 metres from the Tasman Highway, Bangor Wine & Oyster Shed is a farm-gate-style destination offering a mouth-watering marriage: the Dunbabin family's wine and the Gray family's oysters.

Both families are multi-generational farming families from Dunalley who have diversified their historic sheep properties to grow new products. These down-to-earth folk would love for you to visit and connect with the history, people and produce that make their home so special.

For some 16 years, the Grays have been oyster farming in the cool clean waters of Norfolk Bay. And as you sit back with a freshly shucked beauty, you'll understand why these oysters are sought after across the world. What's more, Bangor Vineyard surrounds the shed, so you're spoilt for choice when it comes to an accompanying drop – pinot noir, pinot gris or chardonnay?

The building sits high on the hill of historically significant Bangor, which just happens to be the only place where Abel Tasman came ashore in Tasmania. It's little surprise then that Bangor is rich with history and stories across its 15,000 acres.

The Grays and Dunbabins invite you to a stay a while – shift back a gear into their pace of living. Wander the gift store and you'll find treasures made and carved by locals, inspired by their surrounds. Plus, you'll enjoy old-fashioned value when you purchase wine and oysters direct from the hands of the makers and growers.

There are no food miles at Bangor. What you eat and drink is harvested directly from the scene rolling out beyond the cellar door. Around these parts there's country smiles and a local spirit that will make you feel like moving in to the neighbourhood.

For 364 days a year, wine and oysters and charm are open to enjoy at Bangor. You only have to read the wine labels to get a sense of the stories that will unfold during a visit …

Jimmy's Hill Pinot Gris

Rising a commanding 1002 ft, Jimmy's Hill is Bangor's highest point and one of Tasmania's convict era semaphore stations. With a simple hut for shelter, Jimmy, the rugged bushman who called the remote outpost home, maintained a vigilant eye on adjacent stations, standing by to relay messages.

1830 Chardonnay

In 1830 John Dunbabin, convicted of horse stealing, was transported to Van Diemen's Land. Having narrowly escaped the hangman's noose, he was determined to make the most of his opportunities. Through sheer hard work, John earned his freedom and bought his own land, paving the way for five generations of farming at Bangor.

Captain Spotswood Pinot Noir

Captain John Spotswood, a retired army officer, was the first settler to be granted land at what was to become Bangor, including the land where Bangor's vineyard now stands. Early accounts record that he rather enjoyed a drink, and we expect he would have fancied a glass of this pinot noir bearing his name.

Abel Tasman Pinot Noir

"It behoves us to thank God Almighty with grateful hearts" were the words recorded by Abel Tasman on sailing into a tranquil harbour off Bangor's coastline on 1 December 1642. After an arduous voyage across the unforgiving expanse of the Indian Ocean, he was the first European to set foot upon Tasmania's shores. So let's raise a glass to Abel Tasman and the island named in his honour.

TASMAN PENINSULA

East Coast

TIPS FROM THOSE WHO LIVE HERE
East Coast

> It's not every place on earth you can stand on an open plain while up to 40 wombats graze around you. A Noah's Ark of sorts, Maria Island is wombat heaven.

> "When we go surfing in Bicheno we occasionally get a crayfish from the fish shop at the gulch and a bottle of Tassie Wine and sit up on the hill and watch the sunset."

> Hunting for diamonds on Flinders Island – of the Killiecrankie kind. There's a place there known as The Docks that you'll never want to leave.

> Some may go to Flinders in search of Killicrankie Diamonds, but for me, The Docks were my self-created treasure hunt.

EAST COAST

> Who enjoys a "shut the gate behind you" road into a lush part of Tassie? Brockley Estate in Buckland, owned by Julian and Chax, is one such place. And your Spanish host Chax serves up a very delicious Paella.

> Flinders Island – a treasure more should explore. Chat to a local and they may just point you in the direction of The Docks. The day I walked this coastal stretch I was overcome. Rocky outcrops were capped with bright orange lichen. Walking around each revealed a new secret cove just for me. And like the pages of a book, I just had to keep rounding outcrops to lay eyes on the next patch of paradise.

Bay of Fires Lodge walk*

The lines of a cuttlefish tell the story of its years. Every line is a day and a dark line spells a moment of immense stress. Our Bay of Fires guide concludes the fish in her hands has enjoyed a "stress free life." I'm captivated. Further up the beach, as if opening a window to its soul, I break open another. Staring back are translucently clear lines of relaxed living. Lucky little fish. As I look up, I realise why. Before me is an intoxicating scene.

A Tasman Sea of turquoise rolls into white sands and smooth boulders are topped with a sprinkling of fiery orange. It is nature in her most decorated mood. And there's not a human in sight; not a footprint to follow. It's supposed to be a four-day walk and I begin by standing motionless.

Our cosy group of eight are trekking some 30 kilometres on the Bay of Fires Lodge Walk, along the fringe of Mount William National Park in remote northeast Tasmania. Hailed regularly as one of the hottest destinations on earth, one could anticipate a walk here might be special. But it's not until I abandon my boots and hit the sand that I feel the magic myself. Punctuated by happy chatter among new friends, we cover nine kilometres on day one to reach Forester Beach Camp, nestled in a dune swale. I watch on as guides Kia and Bella are first to disappear into the clear waves. For a moment I disregard thoughts of chilly Tassie waters, popping up beside them like a surprised seal, feeling invigorated.

We rise early to wander over the softest marsupial lawns. Here the guides talk about our environment with the type of innate love normally reserved for your mother. It's a contagious passion that sees more than one of us duck off the path to collect a castaway beer can. Somehow this walk instils the responsibility without words.

After we round the most eastern tip of Tassie, home to stately Eddystone Lighthouse (looking out to sea since 1889), the Bay of Fires really turns up the heat. Stretches of pure white seem endless, secret coves are trumped by the next, and I'm forced to surrender the camera to see this spectacle through both my eyes. Reaching Aboriginal middens, we are reminded of the region's past. "We've been here just eight generations or so," begins Kia, "while the Aborigines foraged for shellfish, dived for seals and hunted mutton birds for some 1500 generations before us, right here." I look down at the darkish sand where campfires lit the eyes of early European explorers, giving rise to the region's name. As I imagine the hub of activity in this isolated corner of Tasmania; it's a silent reminder of those who walked before us.

Further along, when we catch a glimpse of the lodge blending quietly into the landscape, our pace quickens. It promises a footbath, three courses of chef-designed Tasmanian goodness and a hot shower. The architecturally elegant lodge with its commanding deck 40 metres above the sea touches so lightly one almost feels suspended above the

landscape. Inside, cheery guides work like fairies, fluttering about topping glasses with local wine, so intent on making your stay special you just want to tuck them to bed after their 16-hour days.

Commitment to sustainability is somehow balanced effortlessly with five-star dining and luxuries. Yes they're composting toilets and there's no pointed tip on your toilet paper, but where can you laze back in a pink-hazed bathtub of rosella goodness, breathing in salty views? Or in my case, enjoy a head massage where Celia's hands elevate you to a new world of calmness. This is five stars with a thousand stars above.

On day three we set off amongst tall Peppermint gums, to arrive at Ansons River. We slip into double kayaks and a gentle rhythm as we paddle toward Ansons Bay. In fact, so leisurely I barely notice when Bella and I run aground on a weed bed. We are gently eased back into civilisation with a private visit to Apogee Vineyard. It's like wandering into the tool shed of renowned winemaker Andrew Pirie, glimpsing the disgorging process and hand-crafted care afforded to each bottle. Apogee means '"highest point", a fitting end to a walk that moves you to a pinnacle of relaxation usually reserved for local cuttlefish. ●

The details

The walk includes return transfers from Launceston, three nights accommodation, all meals and non-alcoholic beverages, some Tasmanian wines, National Park pass, use of a backpack and Gortex jacket, and two qualified guides. Visit **taswalkingco.com. au** to also find out about the Wineglass Bay Sail Walk.

*First appeared in Luxury Travel magazine Autumn 2014

Maria Island Walk

They tell me he's a commoner. I peer at him and for some reason I'm fixed by his gaze. He's unmoving in a way that forces me to mirror him. I'm pulled into his moment of infectious calm. Perhaps the cosy group of 10 on this Maria Island Walk are wondering why my legs are sticking out of nearby bushes.

But what that common wombat taught me during our intimate encounter is far from common for most of us. He whispered the power of stillness without batting a lazy eyelid, on an island that quietens the soul.

We're journeying some 40 kilometres across Australia's only island national park just east of Tasmania. A haven for rare wildlife, sweeping isolated beaches and convict heritage, this island promises much.

In fitting style, we set foot from boat to sand precisely where French explorers did over 200 years before. Like luminaries, we wander down the gangway onto an entirely desolate beach. But no sooner do I stake my own flag in this shimmering corner of the world, we are whisked away to a gourmet lunch and later to Casuarina Beach camp.

The afternoon is spent dwarfed by towering eucalypts en route to Haunted Bay, where waves tumble against fiery-orange rocks. As I peek into burrows of wide-eyed penguins in a hauntingly-beautiful bay I wonder how the landscape could trump this first side trip. But it does, over and over again.

It seems our guides Ben and Nikki don't reserve candlelit dinners for special occasions. Out here, every night deserves it, regardless of whether it's your 60th or you're rejoicing in those magic fairy guides whipping up three-course dinners as if they have a sous chef tucked out the tent's back zip.

China plates and candelabras sit before us. Tonight's three courses begin with black olive tapenade, vine-ripened tomatoes and basil bruschetta, stir-fried Spring Bay scallops generously swirled into soba noodles for main, and summer-berry pudding with King Island cream, complemented with Springvale Chardonnay and other smooth-flowing local wines.

It's the first of several nights tucked under the familiar wing of Ben and Nikki's shepherding, as 10 strangers promptly become friends. Two doctors go as far as sharing a dinner-table "blankey" in a show of man-affection that begins a tune of rich laughter late into the evening.

It's a dappling of light through the forest that wakes me, along with a chorus of wattlebirds chattering about the beaches we'll walk on day two. They seem beyond excited about the prospect of sharing them with us. I soon realise why local Aborigines termed them "vomit birds", but they're still more endearing than my alarm clock.

We cover a good 12 kilometres on a day that reveals the beginnings of Maria Island's history. We reach a dining room of a different kind, a midden belonging to the Tyreddeme people, who lived for thousands of years feasting on seals, crayfish, oysters and abalone.

We reach the generous shade of macrocarpa trees at Point Lesueur by lunch time, where narrow 19th century convict cells murmur another chapter. Abel Tasman sailed by in 1642, and after an era of French exploration Maria witnessed two convict periods between 1825 and 1850.

As we tuck into our gourmet lunch, at our backs the cells remind us of a time where confinement that pre-dates Port Arthur was reality for about 400 lonely souls. It's a sobering thought, as we take in the very same view, across an island of such majesty.

In place of restrained convicts are all types of wandering locals. There's the endangered forty-spotted pardalote and the world's second-rarest breed of goose, the Cape Barren variety, who crabbily squawk if you enter their "peaceful territory" with too much rigour. And of course, there are those charming wombats.

Although I'm told they can run up to 45 clicks, equivalent to an Olympic sprinter, I don't see many heading for a starting line on their smooth marsupial-lawn carpet. The nocturnal fellows seem much happier grazing, and keeping a watchful eye over the Tasmanian devils that were recently moved here to form an insurance population.

It is hoped this translocation project will assist against the deadly facial tumour disease that wiped out nearly 80 per cent of the mainland Tasmanian devil population. Although we saw only footprints as evidence of their presence, news is positive as 27 healthy devils are happily breeding and feeling very much at home on Maria.

Night two is spent at White Gums camp, where once again a banquet of barbecued quail and lamb cutlets emerge, seemingly from the still night air. Bream Creek Pinot, snappy ginger beer and chilled regional whites fill glasses on a deck where boots are kicked off and replaced by animated chatter about the day's adventures.

Curled up in sturdy canvas havens, we wake to the rolling waves of Four Mile Beach, sparkling mint-green in the morning light. I can't help but raise an eyebrow over my steaming warm coffee as one lady proudly chimes, "I got my nudie swim in this morning."

It's little surprise this very same lady climbed 620 metres to summit Bishop and Clerk the following day with two knees not her own; a feat any surgeon would raise his own brow at, just six months after surgery.

Day three we are treated to the Painted Cliffs, a spectacle well worth getting wet boots for as Ben guides us round a corner, edged by imposing tides. This rippling past showcases an island where fossils believed to be 260 million years old are found. As we tread lightly across this history, only passing dolphins can pull me back to the present.

But as if the island could not get any better, the Maria Island Walk (owned and operated by a passionate local family) leaves the best until last. Climbing the summit of Bishop and Clerk, named for its likeness to churchmen, had to be the highlight for me. After clambering across rock screes that would make any wise person balk at the sight, we are rewarded with a view that has all of us unwilling to leave our perch.

And a lofty, narrow perch it is. It's the type of summit that makes our "blankey doctor" scream as Nikki backs closer to a sheer dolerite cliff edge just to get us all in the photo. The day has gifted us with clear blue skies that meet the famous Hazards Mountains and a 270-degree Maria spectacle. From here, we can relish in the ground we have covered as chocolate is dropped into grateful palms.

This member of the Great Walks of Australia has a grand finale for us though.

We spend the final night in colonial Bernacchi House at Darlington, once home to Italian entrepreneur Diego Bernacchi. He set about transforming the island in the early 1800s. Within those walls we hear tales of his charismatic ways, swaying investors into supporting his vineyards, silkworm and cement works, all failed ventures delivered with grand industrial promise.

This final evening we are spoilt – a verandah overlooking the lavender, a real bed and of course another gourmet feast in the formal dining room, topped with an impromptu birthday cake for one special guest. We eat like kings and feel as such following our first hot shower in three days.

In the morning we can choose to head off to the fossils, explore Darlington or relax with a good book. I choose to wander the nearby area with tired feet and stumble across a story of one Irish prisoner by the name of William Smith O'Brien, sent to Maria in 1849. A far cry from our chirpy huddle preparing for a final champagne lunch, this poor bloke tried to befriend possums to keep him company on cold lonely nights.

It's at the end of our trip that our loyal guides finally put down their 28 kilo packs, ever filled with fresh food, water and safety gear to support our lavishly lighter equivalents. They do so because it's time to leap off the jetty. At first mention of this amusing farewell, I dismissively chuckle. But as guests strip down and guides line the jetty's edge, I realise they're serious.

Still hugging my warm fleece and guarding my camera close, as ammunition to oppose any threat of being tossed over, I smile sensibly beside the few left on the jetty. After swimming around our privately chartered boat, I see two salty fingers appear in front of Ben, signalling round two. Just as the English lady beside me politely asks if I'd considered joining them, it hits me. Without hesitation, I jump in, drawn by the shrieks of chilled joy below. I am fully clothed, complete with socks. But as I wade across to the ladder with a smile as wide as a Bishop and Clerk view, I know it's the perfect end to an unforgettable trip.

It appears the brochure is right, these four days do last a lifetime. I know this when I look around the boat on our 40 minute return to the fishing village of Triabunna. As we ride the waves, I see tired, content smiles on every face. It's a silent, rolling confirmation of the experience we collectively hold. And it's nice. It's nice for those four days to feel what the common wombat has always known – that life's no race unless you're barrelling to an Olympic finish line. ●

Words and images by Alice Hansen

Where: Maria Island, a 40 minute boat ride from Triabunna on Tasmania's east coast

When: Daily from 1 October – 1 May (subject to availability)

What: A four-day guided walk with a maximum of 10 guests and two guides

mariaislandwalk.com.au

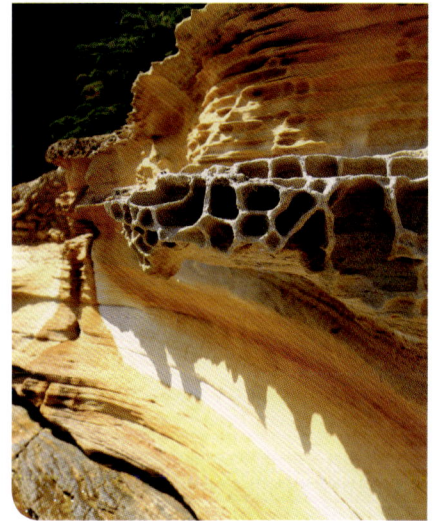

MARIA ISLAND WALK
Maria Island
mariaislandwalk.com.au

Set on a beautiful island national park this outstanding four-day guided walk is a delightful blend of rare Tasmanian wildlife, fascinating history and tranquillity. Small groups of just 10 guests and two friendly guides explore this remarkable island by day and then each night relax with candlelit dining and elegant accommodation. The first two nights are spent in exclusive wilderness camps and the final night in Bernacchi House at the world heritage convict settlement of Darlington. Guests carry only a light pack of 8kg all-inclusive. The all inclusive trip starts and finishes in Hobart and the season runs October to April.

EAST COAST

Freycinet Adventures

Camping in the wilderness. Sipping Tassie wine. Paddling in cool clear waters. Bobbing in the water below bright pink granite peaks. It's the type of experience made for a glossy brochure – and with Freycinet Adventures it'll set you back less than $300. Plus, if you're under five you're as free as the resident dolphins.

They call it the Ultimate Weekender and it's a fairly good description of what's in store. Two days of expedition-style kayaking around the Freycinet Peninsula, this fully-catered tour launched in 2013, in response to demand for longer trips. The backdrop doesn't get much more spectacular, and as visitors from across the globe follow the path up to the Wineglass Bay lookout, few get to experience the region from a kayak seat.

With its relaxed pace the Ultimate Weekend serves up a good dose of kayaking (3–4 hours each day), a dash of walking and an overnight at the private camp at Hazards Beach. Here you can snorkel, swim or sink your toes into the white sands with a good book and some local cheese.

The locally-owned business also offers popular twilight and morning kayak trips as well – running for three hours. With a maximum of 12 guests you're assured a cosy group and intimate interpretation of Freycinet National Park.

You'll be rewarded with morning or afternoon tea on a secluded beach beneath the Hazards peaks and more than your share of history, ranging from the rich archaeological evidence of Aboriginal occupation to the early French explorers. Middens, old mine shafts, abandoned farmers' huts and whalers' camps can be found dotted along the coastline, so be ready for your trusted guide to share a peninsula tale or two on the journey. ●

2 Freycinet Drive, Coles Bay
freycinetadventures.com.au

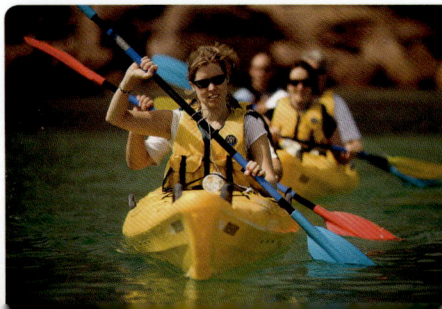

Wineglass Bay Cruises

There's something very special about a Wineglass Bay Cruise – and that's Ras. He's the dolphin-spotting sea dog that bounds up and down the boat, peering into the blue in search of his finned friends. He'll bark and let you know when he's had luck. "First Mate Ras" is incredibly cute.

But it's not just Ras that makes a cruise with Duncan and Irene unforgettable. It's the whole friendly approach – from the friendly smiles on arrival, to Ras and your experienced skipper Duncan with his vast knowledge of this ancient coastline.

The Trip

We explore the Freycinet Peninsula's stunning coastline in a way few visitors can. Discovering the natural and human history of this extraordinary place as we cruise beneath ruggedly-beautiful pink granite cliffs that rise straight up from the Tasman Sea, skirting forested capes and discovering hidden sea-swept bays. En route we encounter some of the Peninsula's marine birdlife including white-bellied sea eagles and huge flocks of albatross, gannets and short-tailed shearwaters.

Shortly after we anchor in Wineglass Bay and are served up some of Tasmania's finest produce, the lavish "Tasmanian ploughman's lunch". Ras keeps an ever-watchful eye for pods of sleek dolphins, cavorting seals and whales.

Just after departing Wineglass Bay Ras barks into action and we are treated to a remarkable feeding frenzy of dolphins and seals working together to hunt a huge school of fish. The crew explain that data from wildlife observations is gathered and sent to the Nature Conservation Branch of Tasmania to assist with their research and increase local awareness.

All we had to do though is soak up the scenery on our return journey, and give Ras a friendly pat every now and then for his hard work. After all, we're in his office. ●

wineglassbaycruises.com

EAST COAST

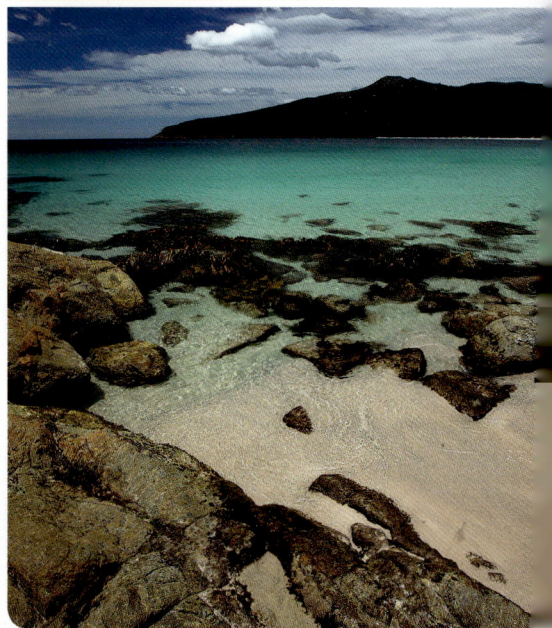

EAST COAST CRUISES
Tribunna Marina – Departure Point
eastcoastcruises.com.au

Maria Island is an expanse of brilliant wilderness, pristine beaches, protected marine habitats, mountain views, world-heritage convict history and isolated recreation. These famous cruise and walk day tours take you to visit the best of Maria Island in just one day. Enjoy a buffet lunch beside the Ile Des Phoques (Island of Seals), sip a Tasmanian sparkling wine inside giant sea caves, relax as you drift the boat aside cliff-top waterfalls and put the anchor down in a secluded bay with three kilometers of pure white sand. In the afternoon you'll be immersed in the history of the Darlington convict settlement. Guides walk you through beautifully-preserved buildings, and if you're lucky you might get a portrait with the local wombats!

FREYCINET ADVENTURES
2 Freycinet Drive, Coles Bay
freycinetadventures.com.au

Freycinet Adventures is a multi-award-winning ecotourism business delivering a range of guided sea kayaking tours on the east coast of Tasmania. Since 1996 the business has been delivering sea kayaking experiences with three key things in mind – passion, people and place. Freycinet Adventures is respected as one of the leading providers of sea kayaking experiences in Tasmania, reflected by its inclusion in the Tasmanian Tourism Awards Hall of Fame for Adventure Tourism. They aim to enable people to step out of the everyday and experience natural adventure in Tasmania's spectacular coastal environment.

WINEGLASS BAY CRUISES
Coles Bay, East Coast
wineglassbaycruises.com

Step aboard the luxury catamaran Schouten Passage II for an unforgettable four-hour cruise, taking you from the gentle shores of Coles Bay to the world-famous Wineglass Bay. Cruising the Freycinet Peninsula, you'll experience stunning scenery, abundant wildlife and a rare, intimate perspective on one of Tasmania's most extraordinary places. At anchor in Wineglass Bay, you'll have time to absorb the true peace of this place, as you enjoy a Tasmanian ploughman's lunch. Dolphins, seals, albatross, sea eagles, and whales on their annual migration from September to December are regular visitors to the cruise. Let's not forget Ras, the world-famous dolphin-spotting dog.

EAST COAST

Events

tailor a reason to come

Whip your clothes off for the annual **nude swim** – or slip into the dressed crowd and enjoy **Dark Mofo** in all its colourful, wintery madness.

Head for Hobart when it's most alive – as the **Sydney to Hobart** yachts cross the line and the **Taste Festival** is humming.

With so much water around us, the **Wooden Boat Festival** is particularly special and celebrates our maritime heritage.

Ten Days on the Island – worth every day of it and **Festival of Voices** gets us all chanting by the bonfire!

Adventure
FURTHER AFIELD

World's highest commercial abseil

DON'T LOOK DOWN

At any crossroads, a good friend will sit by your side and tell you "the only way is up". But I'm telling you, the best way is straight down. I had been suffering a serious case of writer's block for months – not fun when income is attached to hitting creative pen to paper. Finally, I found myself in a desperate state: I couldn't keep going like this. Not if I didn't want to spend the rest of my days living on noodles.

My invitation back into the land of the living begins with a small hand gesture. Tap tap, goes his hand on the rail, followed by a very casual, "up you hop." It is as relaxed as a blackjack player tapping the table for another card but it signals something far more ominous.

I look down at the rain-splattered rail and wonder, again, why the hell I'd thought this was the answer. In the sideways misty rain of south-western Tasmania, my new-found mate – a Kiwi instructor with impenetrably dark sunglasses – is asking me to literally swing a leg over a near-shoulder high guard rail at the Gordon Dam.

My next task? To abseil 140 metres down the world's highest commercial abseil. It's a few metres higher than standing atop Sydney Harbour Bridge, and holds back 30 times the amount of water than the harbour itself.

Moments earlier, I'd watched an American boldly climb over the rail. Moments before that, he'd shared the story of his fight with a shark in the waters off Mexico, in which he lost half his calf – I'd reckoned the Gordon Dam Abseil would be a walk in the park for him. But as I bid him farewell and he went over the edge, the fear in his eyes was like nothing I'd ever seen.

Giant round saucers stared ahead, a mix of focus and fear, as expletives flew. Then … he was gone.

For some reason, I feel compelled to declare that I won't dare swear. I step up. Significant instructions of how to release the rope in my right hand on descent are met with my nervous but misinterpreted nod: they think I'm ready to do this. All of a sudden I'm on the wrong side of the rail.

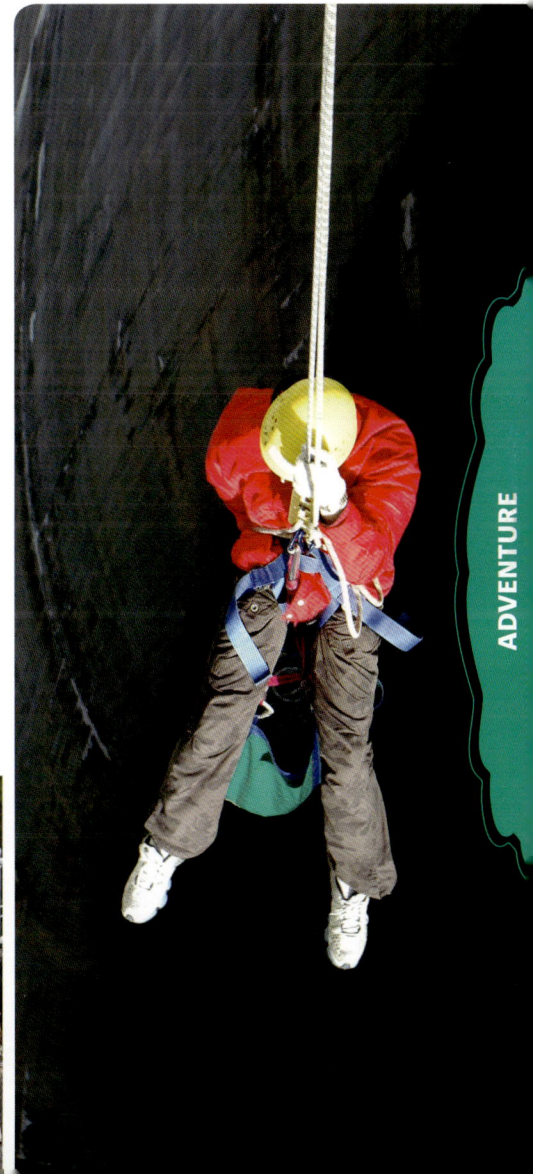

Then I do something incredibly foolish: I tilt my head downward.

"The one thing you mustn't do is look down," one of the instructors, a young Scottish girl, had warned as I climbed over. As for the promise of not swearing ... the Gordon Dam has suddenly become the best amphitheatre for every bad word I can muster.

My lovely New Zealand pal is telling me to take my feet off the wall. Sitting in mid-air 140 metres up, staring at an 11-millimetre thick "life line", I reach a new point where even naughty words can't pass my lips. I fall silent with terror. I'd heard one lady had completed the journey from top to bottom with her eyes closed. Apparently she was terrified of heights (can't understand why). As I inch my way down, centimetres at a time with my eyes on the wall, her method suddenly seems quite appealing.

But the moment I clench them shut, a cheery, "ah, look! You're spinning around," comes from above. "Take a look at the glorious view." I open one eye and to my distress see that I have full view of just how horrifically high up I am. Yes, the view is spectacular – rocks ... trees ... water and stuff ... but I am focused on survival.

By this stage I am so terrified that my hands are shaking uncontrollably, unable to control my speed – I have to rely on my mate upstairs for that. He seems to be enjoying my shrieks as he gently controls my descent. Because of the curvature of the dam, I'm dangling about

15 metres out from the wall. It's a lonely life midway down ... and eerily silent.

It's amazing what goes through your mind at times like this. I am soaked to my skin. I am near tears. I start imagining that I'm an ambulance officer, forced to do this to save someone's life. It makes more sense to be suspended from a life-ending height for some better purpose.

But while the weather and dread is bleak, it is equally beautiful. This is the south-west in one of her wildest moods – a mix of relentless rain, unforgiving cold and foreboding fog. As the rope decides to spin me round again, revealing the breathtaking panorama, I realise this moment is incredibly special.

I look out to the craggy cliffs, the dense forest, look up to the encouraging instructors, and I feel a sense of pride. I've accomplished something. I am in careful, trusted, safe hands. I have conquered fear.

It is time to enjoy the journey. And it is spectacular. For a moment, I breathe in some of the freshest air on the planet. For a moment, I absorb the beauty of the surrounds, and the manmade commitment to this region. For a moment, I feel more alive than I've felt in years. For a moment ... hell, I am still far too high to survive if the rope falls short.

But when I do finally touch down there is that American, still as wide-eyed as I'd left him up top but this time with a sense of rush and bewilderment. We would have had a congratulatory handshake, but contact is difficult when your hands are still shaking so immensely you can't unhook yourself from the soggy, nappy-type contraption we're both still wearing.

Was it worth the guide-rail leap? More than anything. Would I be caught climbing it again? Not likely. But one thing is for sure – those 11 millimetres of rope will send you on a journey that will test your spirit, challenge your courage, and leave you buoyed with the knowledge that you can tackle anything ... even a blank page. ●

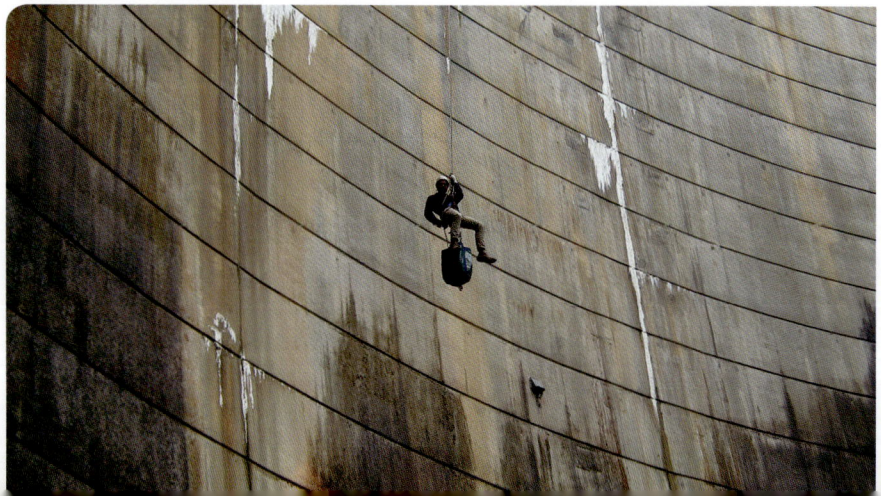

The details

GETTING THERE

Allow one day for the abseil. The drive from central Hobart to south-west Tasmania takes approximately 2.5 hours each way (the drive is exquisite and is included in the cost). But if time is limited a helicopter can be chartered taking approximately 45 minutes each way. www.rotorlift.com.au

NEED TO KNOW

Aardvark Adventures is the only company that operate abseils from Gordon Dam. The cost is $210 per person and includes guides, ropes, equipment, safety gear, insurance, photography package and a certificate to prove your bravery. Bring warm clothes as weather can become moody in the south-west wilderness. Trips run all year round and require a minimum of just two people in order to go ahead. www.aardvarkadventures.com.au

HOT TIP

Lake Pedder is well worth a visit en route. To walk around this once glacial lake and pink quartz beach has been described as "walking with the gods". Protests erupted worldwide when the lake was flooded to create a hydro-electric scheme but it's still very beautiful.

Words by Alice Hansen
This story first appeared in Australian Traveller Magazine

Southwest Wilderness Camp, Port Davey

There aren't many places left in the world where the silence is audible. In the south-west wilderness of Tasmania, it's easy to feel like you're the last person standing. And for the first time, Par Avion has opened the doors to a luxury standing camp, inviting you to enjoy three days in remote wilderness.

Lightly positioned on the shores of Bathurst Harbour, the camp has no walking track access and is exclusive to a cosy group of no more than eight. It's your base to explore 800 metre mountain peaks rising from the sea, the endangered orange-bellied parrots, untouched waterways on your own private boat, and breathe some of the freshest air on the planet.

Getting to your camp aboard a twin engine islander aircraft, of course, is half the fun. On day one Par Avion takes off from Cambridge Airport, letting you bid farewell to the city of Hobart before following the rugged southern coastline to Melaleuca. Home to countless shipwrecks, the coastline and vast wilderness below offer a sense of the remoteness to come – your pilot will point out the natural highlights including Federation Peak and the Western Arthur Range on your return flight.

Where have you landed? In 4500 square kilometres of Southwest National Park, a lost world where you can explore world heritage listed wilderness and by evening share tall tales over a glass of Tasmanian wine and local fare. It's a luxurious contrast to the hardships of Deny King, a tin miner who lived self-sufficiently in this far-flung corner of the

world for over half a century. On day one you'll visit the home of this legend and also hear stories of the Aboriginal Needwonee people before boarding a private boat for transport to the camp.

After lunch it's time to explore a harbour three times the size of Sydney Harbour. By boat you'll visit the Celery Top Islands, walk through temperate rainforest and to the top of Mount Beattie if you're keen, before returning for quality Tasmanian food and wine and the inviting fluffy doona of your boutique hut.

On day two, head off by boat through the Bathurst Narrows to Balmoral Beach – nothing like whipping off your shoes on a pristine beach. Visit the grave site of an early explorer who was in search of a potential location for the "New Jerusalem" – a place for the persecuted Jews of World War II to call home.

Following lunch, view the stunning white quartzite cliffs of Port Davey and an ancient Aboriginal ochre cave.

On the final day, those who have been eyeing off 771 metre high Mount Rugby can climb to its peak above the Bathurst Narrows, a five-hour return walk. Other more relaxed options include Cox Bight Beach or exploring an ancient Huon pine forest before the 4pm return flight home.

Par Avion also offers flights to plenty of other Tasmanian destinations including Wineglass Bay, Port Arthur and Maria Island. For those looking to learn to take to the skies themselves, Par Avion also provides flight training. If you're after adventure, hop on board. ●

Par Avion Wilderness Tours
Phone (03) 6248 5390
paravion.com.au

"The south-west wilderness will move you. It will stay with you. There are few places that have captured my imagination and brought me to a complete standstill the way the south-west did. Having enjoyed a day trip with Par Avion to this part of the world, I can only imagine staying through nightfall and waking up in this place. A few more pages to go of Deny King's book and I'll be ready."

PUMPHOUSE POINT – *Lake St Clair*

In the middle of Tasmania, on the southern hemisphere's deepest lake, awaits a brand-new wilderness experience – Pumphouse Point.

Walk deep into the fjord-like surrounds of Lake St Clair, explore the giant myrtle forests, tread softly on the moss-covered understorey and forget the world you left behind. At day's end, return to the sanctuary of the Pumphouse to share tables and tales with fellow guests by a crackling fire. Surrounded by some of the most dramatic natural landscape on the planet, the scene is set for your new favourite memory.

pumphousepoint.com.au

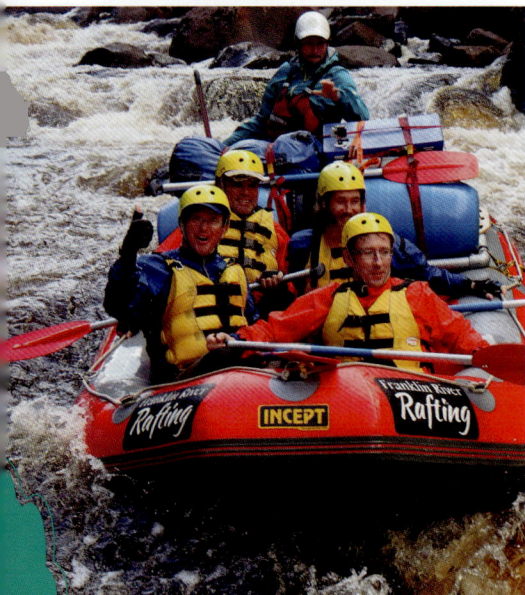

FRANKLIN RIVER RAFTING
franklinriverrafting.com

The Franklin River is one of the last truly wild rivers on earth. It is a complex system of breathtaking scenery, powerful energy and moments of utter tranquility, threading its way through the World Heritage Area. There are few environments in the world as ancient, untouched or majestic. Franklin River Rafting specialises in uninterrupted eight- and 10-day whitewater rafting tours, and is owned and operated by the guides that take you down the river. Elias, Franzi and their friends will share their intimate knowledge and love of the Franklin with you during this unparalleled experience. No previous rafting experience is necessary. A basic level of fitness, a thirst for adventure and a love for the outdoors is all you require.

AARDVARK ADVENTURES
Statewide
aardvarkadventures.com.au

Based in Tasmania, Aardvark can provide abseiling, caving, whitewater rafting and kayaking adventures, as well as team building activities, conference tours and school outdoor programs. Challenge yourself at the world's highest commercial abseil, or raft through the rainforests in the south-west World Heritage Area. Explore Tasmania's hidden underground world of caves and tunnels. Whether it be tackling the rapids of a white water rafting route or enjoying a pleasant kayak paddle, Aardvark Adventures can offer specially tailored packages that will suit you. They provide a dynamic range of recreational activities all year round.

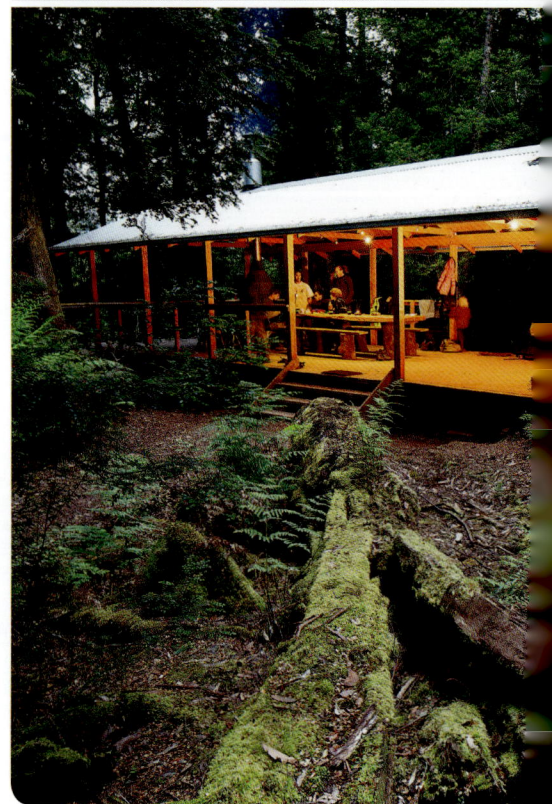

TARKINE TRAILS
tarkinetrails.com.au

Twelve years ago Tarkine Trails pioneered tourism in the Tarkine region in Tasmania's north-west. Their goal is to provide a positive economic alternative to the resource extraction industry that was devastating — and continues to devastate — the area, the largest temperate rainforest in the southern hemisphere. Creating a positive future that connects people with the Tarkine is their mission. Join them for a journey into the ancient Tarkine and know that your holiday helps to keep it that way.

ADVENTURE

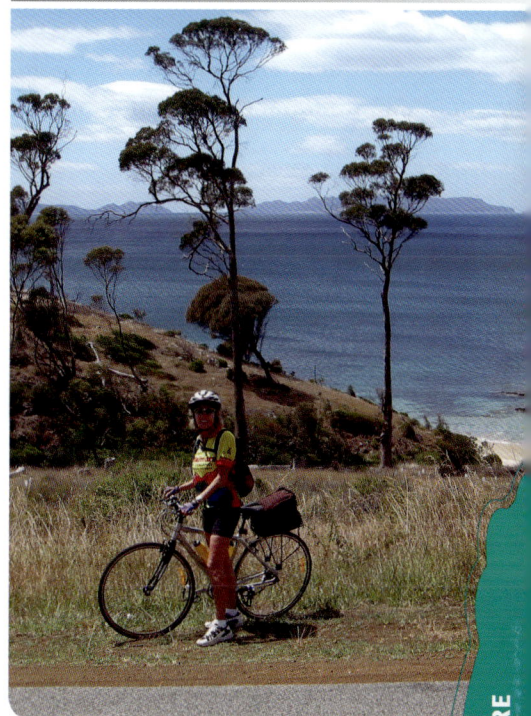

ADVENTURE

CRADLE MOUNTAIN CANYONS
cradlemountaincanyons.com.au

Launch yourself off waterfalls, abseil down cliffs and shoot through nature's waterslides. Or take an easier option and float along seeing the world from the point of view of a platypus. Canyoning is a must-do for lovers of adventure at Cradle Mountain. It involves putting on a wetsuit and helmet and swimming, floating, abseiling, walking and jumping your way through a section of river – like whitewater rafting without the raft. Cradle Mountain Canyons is the only business in Tasmania offering guided canyoning tours. No experience necessary – just an appetite for adventure. Tours depart from the Cradle Mountain Visitor Centre.

PAR AVION
paravion.com.au

Par Avion can take you to some of the most stunning and distant corners of wild Tasmania. Take an unforgettable three-day trip, exploring the incredible waterways and wilderness of Bathurst Harbour, some of Tasmania's most inaccessible wilderness. Or take a flight to Maria Island, landing at Darlington where you'll then board a vessel and see the remarkable sea caves of the Isle De Phoques. Sound exciting? Par Avion can take you there. They fly daily into the Southwest National Park of Tasmania and to the east coast, as well as offer general charter and tourist flights statewide. If you're an avid bushwalker, they'll happily deliver you to Melaleuca or somewhere equally stunning to begin your journey.

PEDALTOURS
pedaltours.com

Since 1985 Pedaltours has offered guided cycle tours. Explore Tasmania at a leisurely pace, staying at the best lodges and dining well. There are rest days in Freycinet, Launceston at Strahan. Tours are 8, 9 or 16 day or they will arrange a custom tour to suit. Tours are fully supported – luggage carried and everyone cycles as little or as much as they wish. They have very good quality lightweight bikes available in a wide range of sizes. Local guides add a personal touch with their extensive knowledge. The Pedaltours team is dedicated to bringing you the bicycle holiday of a lifetime.

Cook
like a local

islandmenu.com.au

Island Menu is a food and photography blog written by two friends – Samuel Shelly and Catherine Miller – with a strong focus on the use of wonderful fresh Tasmanian produce available. With *Island Menu* they hope to share recipes that are simple yet full of flavor and present them in thier photographs in a way that is both sincere and honest.

Sam, tell us about yourself, a little of your background and how *Island Menu* came to be.

I am a photographer based in Hobart and I love fishing and cooking. Catherine and I have been friends since high school and alway's had similar interests – cooking and photography being two of them. I think *Island Menu* was spawned out of a boozey winter's afternoon at Knoppies [Knopwood's Retreat in Salamanca Place].

What is the inspiration behind *Island Menu* and what do you hope to offer your loyal following?

We always used to talk a lot but never did anything about it. By creating the blog we thought it might pull us into action. As far as what we hope to offer I would say we want to give people small slices of Tasmania that sit outside your standard tourist attractions.

The blog is a beautiful representation of life in Tassie – what is it you love most about living here?

I love that I don't have to deal with crowds and that we have so much to do right on our doorstep. For example, I worked from home last summer because of our new baby and I spent most lunch times snorkelling and spearing fish out the front of our house – and we are only 10 minutes from the centre of Hobart.

What's been one of the best experiences that you've showcased on your *Island Menu* blog?

I think my tuna trips to Pedra Branca and Mewstone stand out for me.

What is it that you love about fishing off our coastlines?

I think that there is always something different. You can catch sea trout close to Hobart then only 50 kilometres away catch a 100-kilo tuna.

Where do you enjoy going for a bite with friends when you're not cooking?

Smolt

Will you share a local secret with us?

One tip I always give visitors is if you're driving around the state buy produce as you go from farm gates and cellar doors then have a picnic somewhere at the end of the day. I think that is the best way to experience the food down here.

What's your favourite day out?

That would be fishing out in Storm Bay and coming back to our shack at North Bruny and cooking up the catch over a few beers.

CIDER-BATTERED OYSTERS

On the weekend my sister and I took a quick road trip to a mate's oyster farm on Bruny Island. The tide was pretty high so we had to wade out to the racks and with numb hands grab a few for tea.

After trying some oysters with apple a little while ago, I'd been meaning to make some cider batter. The sweetness of the cider means the oysters taste a bit like abalone. You don't really need a dipping sauce as they are already pretty full on, but I did make the one below and it was great.

Ingredients

Two dozen oysters, shucked

Batter

1 cup	apple cider (I used quite a dry one)
1 cup	flour
	Salt
	Canola oil for frying

Sauce

2	egg yolks
2 tsp	Dijon mustard
¾ tsp	white pepper
2 tbsp	apple cider vinegar
250 ml	sunflower seed oil
50 ml	rosemary infused olive oil
	Pinch of salt

Method

1 To make the batter, combine flour and cider into a runny paste and refrigerate for one hour.

2 To make the sauce, combine egg yolks, vinegar, mustard, pepper and salt. Beat slowly with an electric beater and add the oils until the mixture thickens.

3 Fill a medium sized pot with oil and heat to 180 degrees Celsius or just before it starts to smoke (you want it nice and hot).

4 Dip the oysters in the batter and fry until golden.

5 Season and serve.

HOT-SPICED APPLE AND BRANDY DRINK

Sunday morning was magnificent – flat calm on the river and sunny – so we put our driving hats on and went for a Sunday drive down the channel. We stopped at the Woodbridge jetty for a fish, but I didn't even look like catching anything so I soon canned that and went looking for lunch. It is a real larder down there. We found honey, jams, cheese, trout and heaps more. We stopped in at Grandvewe Cheeses for a quick look around – but more on that later.

Coincidentally this week Catherine and I used pretty much the same ingredients to make different things. We have been wanting to do a drink on the site for a while now and being winter this seemed like the perfect option.

Ingredients

- **4** cups of apple Juice
- **1** cinnamon stick
- **3** slithers of ginger (about the size of a 20 cent coin)
- **3** cloves
    Zest of 1 lemon (about 1 strip the length of the lemon)
    Juice of ½ a lemon
- **1 tsp** honey
- **4** decent shots/lugs of brandy

Method

1 Throw everything apart from the brandy into a pot and simmer for 45–60 minutes – or until the flavours of the spices come out.

2 Add the brandy and serve hot.

islandmenu.com.au

LAMB AND ALE PIE WITH JANSSON'S CRUST

After trying Jansson's temptation (basically a potato bake with anchovies through it) in Sweden, the dish has made regular dinner appearances at our place. Ever since, I've wanted to make a shepherd's style pie with Jansson's crust, and this week I finally got around to it.

Ingredients:

700g	lamb cut into large chucks (I used the sinewy part of the leg)
6	small onions, chopped
	A bunch of baby carrots, chopped
1	stick of celery, finely chopped
1 cup	mixed mushrooms (I used oyster, honey brown and shitake)
1	cup ale
1½	cups beef stock
4	tbs flour
2	tbs thyme
3	bay leaves
2	cloves
2	cloves of garlic, finely chopped
	Pepper and salt
	Olive oil
3–4	anchovies, finely chopped
3–4 tbs	grated gruyere
4	waxy potatoes, sliced finely into discs

Method

1 Pre-heat the oven to 150 degrees Celsius.

2 Dust the lamb in seasoned flour and fry in a pot with some hot oil until brown. Set aside in a baking dish.

3 In the same pot used for the lamb, reduce the heat then add the onions, carrots, celery, thyme, bay leaves and cloves. Cook until the onion is a tad translucent, then add the garlic and mushrooms.

4 After the garlic is cooked, add two to three tablespoons of flour and cook out till it coats everything. Add the beer and beef stock. Heat to simmer, then add pepper and salt to taste. Put the mixture in a baking dish with the lamb, then pop it in the oven for about one and a half hours, or until the lamb is tender.

5 Skim the fat off the lamb and place everything into a pie dish. Layer the potato disks in two layers with cheese and anchovies scattered throughout.

6 Finish with some thyme and pepper then put it back in a moderate oven until the potato is cooked and golden. I finish mine off under the grill to get the potatoes nice and crispy.

islandmenu.com.au

MUTTONBIRDS

At the moment I am on holidays at our shack on Bruny Island. The weather hasn't been that kind, nor have the fish, so a lot of time has been spent eating and drinking by the fire. Yesterday, feeling like we needed to do some exercise, we went for a walk and a bit of a cook up.

A while ago I scored some mutton birds off my butcher (there are pretty tight restrictions on harvesting them these days – you can't do it at all in the south of the state). Muttonbirds are sea birds that nest in Tasmania in late summer after a massive migration from the northern hemisphere. You either love or hate mutton birds. They are really strong in flavour; I would describe them as duck crossed with anchovies. They also stink when you cook them – my girlfriend will only let me cook them outside. So it seemed fitting that we took the birds with us on our walk to an old muttonbirding hut.

Cooking

It was perfect out at the hut. We had the whole beach to ourselves. We lit a fire and chucked on some spuds and threw the birds on the grill. When they were cooked we ate them with shots of vodka (whiskey would be better) – this helped cut through the fattiness of the birds. I got this idea from the way the Swedes eat their surströmming (fermented herring) – just with potatoes and schnapps. I remember it being a pretty good way to eat it but that may have been the schnapps talking. What I mainly liked is the way they make a bit of a party or event out of eating the herring – they do the same with their freshwater crayfish. It is something that I think we miss out on a bit here, maybe because we are quite a young country? Anyway as you may have gathered by now this is not really a recipe, more of a way to enjoy these birds.

TUNA NIÇOISE WITH LEMON AND PEPPER MAYONNAISE

Last Sunday was the best day tuna fishing I have ever had.

We left Hobart at 6am and headed south. A few hours later we had the lines in the water and started to troll. I think it only took three minutes and we had a quadruple hook up – was rather tricky with only four of us in the boat. After that we decided that it would be more sensible to run three rods and a while later we went to two. The tuna were coming to the boat thick and fast and it didn't take long for the seals to cotton on to what we were doing – there was quite a bit of tug of war going on. I think my arms are still sore! Once we had got our bag we headed for the shack where we had a cold beer waiting. A perfect day.

I think alone I have eaten about 5kg of tuna this week but I'm still not sick of it. We normally eat it by itself with a bit of soy and wasabi but by the end of the week we decided we needed some vegetables so I made this salad.

Ingredients

300g	fresh Tuna
½ cup	green beans
2	cos lettuce hearts
2 tbsp	capers, roughly chopped
2 tbsp	red onion, finely chopped
3	eggs
2	tomatoes, quartered
4	small waxy potatoes
½ cup	sunflower seed oil
½ cup	olive oil
2	egg yolks
2 tsp	horseradish
2 tsp	white vinegar
	Juice of 2 lemons
3 tsp	cracked black pepper
	Salt to taste

Mayonnaise

In an electric whisk beat the egg yolks, horseradish, pinch of salt, and vinegar. While whisking slowly add the oil. Now add the lemon and pepper to taste.

Salad

1 Soft boil the eggs.

2 Boil the potatoes and blanch the beans and set aside.

3 Break up the cos hearts and dress with a bit of olive oil and salt. Plate up the cos, potatoes, beans, tomatoes and eggs.

4 Season the tuna and sear in a hot pan on all sides – this should only take about 20 seconds on each side. Slice the tuna finely and place on top of the salad. Place the capers and onion on top of the tuna and add a bit of the dressing.

islandmenu.com.au

SMOKED SALMON, STRAWBERRY AND FENNEL TERRINE

A few months ago I met Roger from the Woodbridge Smokehouse. It was winter at the time, so I asked him if I could pop back and take some photos of the smokehouse and surrounding orchard when the weather got a bit better. I finally got around to heading down earlier this week. Jesus it gets light early at the moment – I had to get up at 3.50am to catch the sunrise.

I'm glad I made the effort, it was pretty perfect down there. From the top of the hill you could see right up and down the Channel and over to Bruny Island. After a cup of tea Roger showed me the smokehouse and how it all works – it was really interesting. I got some good tips as my first go at cold smoking was a bit of a balls-up.

Roger's cold smoked salmon is pretty bloody good so normally I would suggest to eat it as is but this is a food blog with recipes sooo ... I thought I would give a terrine of cold smoked salmon and strawberries a crack. I have never made a terrine before so this could have ended in tears but luckily it worked out pretty okay.

Ingredients

Approx 500g of sliced smoked salmon

1/3 cup	goats curd
1/3 cup	sour cream
1½ cups	strawberries
1 cup	fennel tips (if you don't like fennel you can use basil)
	Zest of 1/3 of a lemon
1 tbsp	cracked black pepper
1 tbsp	raspberry vinegar
	Olive oil, fennel tips and raspberry vinegar to serve

To make the terrine

1 Grease and line a terrine dish (I used a loaf tin) with cling wrap.

2 Line the bottom and sides (a fair way up) with salmon.

3 Mix goats curd, sour cream and lemon zest and add a thin layer to the terrine (less is more – you don't want it to be overpowering).

4 Slice the strawberries and mix with the vinegar and add a layer of them and fennel tips to the terrine plus a good hit of black pepper.

5 Add some more of the sour cream mix then another layer of salmon.

6 Now repeat: sour cream, strawberries, fennel, pepper, then sour cream and a layer of salmon.

7 Fold over the sides of salmon onto the final layer then wrap with the lined cling film.

8 Weigh down with some weights and refrigerate for 24 hours.

9 Finish with olive oil and some more vinegar and serve with some rye toast.

INDULGENT CHOCOLATE CAKE WITH AGRARIAN KITCHEN *DULCE DU LECHE*

This Easter we celebrated our friend Rose's 30th birthday at her lodge in the central Tasmanian highlands. It was a very relaxed weekend, a bit of drinking, puzzle-doing, Easter egg eating, and a lot of chats around the fire. Sam caught a two-pound brown trout and Rose's husband Bill cooked us a fantastic Hāngi. Oh yeah and we had snow!

To celebrate the birthday I made my standard chocolate cake, but this time around made it that little bit more indulgent – well it was Easter – by adding in a layer of the Agrarian Kitchen's dulce du leche purchased from their stall at the Mona Market. This stuff is liquid gold and is made from their own goats milk. It's beautifully rich. I'm hooked!

Ingredients

230g	dark chocolate (I use Green & Black 70%)
170g	unsalted butter at room temperature
350g	brown sugar
3	free range eggs, separated
370g	plain flour, sifted
1½	teaspoons bicarb soda
1½	teaspoons baking powder
500ml	skinny milk
2 tsp	vanilla extract

Method

1 Grease and line two 20cm round tins and preheat the oven to 170 degrees Celsius.

2 Melt the chocolate gently and set aside to cool while you work on the next steps.

3 In a large mixing bowl cream the butter and sugar until smooth and pale, then add the egg yolks and beat for several minutes. Add the melted chocolate to the mix and again beat well.

4 Combine the sifted flour, bicarb and baking powder in a separate bowl and add the vanilla extract to the milk in a jug. Add one-third of the flour mix to the creamed butter mix and one-third of the milk mixture, beat until well combined. Repeat this process until all the flour and milk have been added.

5 In a clean bowl beat the egg whites until soft peaks form and gently fold into the cake batter with a metal spoon. Divide the batter between the two cake tins and bake for approximately 40 minutes or until a skewer comes out clean.

6 Leave the cakes in the tins for 10 minutes after removing from the oven to allow to set. Once cool place one cake on a plate, pour some whiskey into a tablespoon and gently pour over evenly into the cake. Allow it to soak in and then cover with a layer of icing and some crushed toasted hazelnuts. Place the second cake on top and once again gently pour another tablespoon of whiskey over the top. Ice and decorate as you wish.

islandmenu.com.au

Icing

175g dark chocolate
225g unsalted butter at room temp
250g icing sugar
1 tbsp skinny milk
1 tsp vanilla extract

1 Gently melt the chocolate and allow to cool slightly.

2 Place the butter, milk, sifted icing sugar and vanilla in a mixing bowl and beat until smooth. Add the melted chocolate and beat again until thick and creamy.

CALAMARI WITH HOMEMADE TARTARE SAUCE

Last weekend we made a trip down to the shack at Bruny Island with a few friends. The weather was perfect so we went and caught a few calamari until the boat decided it didn't want to start. It didn't matter, we already had a feed, so we retired to the deck for a BBQ.

We didn't end up cooking the calamari until we got home but in my mind there is pretty much only one way to cook fresh calamari, and that's to keep it simple – crumbed, shallow fried with homemade tartare. This would have to be about my favourite meal. If you are making this make sure you get southern calamari and not arrow squid – there is a big difference.

Ingredients

1	medium-sized calamari tube cut into rings
1½	cups panko bread crumbs
1	egg
2	egg yolks
	A dash of milk
1 cup	seasoned plain flour

Tartare Sauce

3	egg yolks
2/3 cup	sunflower seed oil
1/3 cup	olive oil
1 heaped tsp	Dijon mustard
	White pepper and salt to taste
1 tbsp	white vinegar
	Juice of half a lemon
1½ tbsp	spring onions, finely chopped
2 tbsp	parsley, finely chopped
1 tsp	tarragon, finely chopped
1 tbsp	dill, finely chopped
2 tsp	preserved lemon peel, finely chopped
2 tbsp	capers, finely chopped
1 tbsp	gherkins, finely chopped

Method

1 Coat squid rings in flour and dust off excess. Then coat in beaten egg and milk mixture and shake off excess. Then coat in breadcrumbs.

2 To make the tartare, in an electric beater combine egg yolks, vinegar, lemon juice, pepper, and mustard. Then very, very slowly add the oils while still whisking. Once all the oil has been added you should have a nice mayonnaise.

3 To the mayonnaise add the onion, parsley, preserved lemon peel, tarragon, dill, capers and gherkins and stir well. Let this sit for an hour or so – it is much better when it has been left to stand.

4 Just before you want to serve, place about 1cm of oil in a frying pan and heat until about 180 degrees Celsius. I find on most stove tops use about three-quarters heat. Fry the rings until just golden on one side and turn until golden on the other, which should take at most 30 seconds on each side. Serve hot with the tartare.

islandmenu.com.au

DEEP-FRIED PERCH WITH PINKEYE, CHORIZO & QUINOA CHIPS AND A SPRING ONION MAYONNAISE

With the fine weather last Sunday we dragged the boat down to Bruny for a spot of fishing. We headed straight for a small reef I have been studying on the charts for some time now. On arrival we were greeted by a seal but I managed to scare him off. We had to work hard for the perch amongst an armada of unwanted fish (and when I say "we" I mean "me" – Lottie was asleep most of the morning).

On Saturday night Catherine and I did a bit of recipe testing. I had some great pinkeye potatoes left over and with the fish that I caught on Sunday, fish and chips had to be on the menu.

I got the idea for the deep fried quinoa from Garagistes – they had it served on some poached calamari – it was pure awesome. I am not a massive fan of going out for tea (my favourite food is a chump chop sandwich in white bread with sauce) but it would have to be the best food in any restaurant that I have eaten. The thing that struck me was the amount of thought that had gone into each recipe.

Ingredients

Chips ────────────

6	pinkeye potatoes
1	chorizo sausage, finely sliced
2	tbsp cooked quinoa
	Mayonnaise
2	egg yolks
1 cup	sunflower oil
1 tsp	Dijon mustard
	Juice of half a lemon
2	capsful of white vinegar
	White pepper
2 tbsp	sour cream
2	spring onions, finely chopped

Fish ────────────

1	perch or any small whole fish
½ cup	plain flour
½ cup	cornflour
1 tbsp	salt
1 tbsp	black pepper

Method

1 To make the mayonnaise add the egg yolks, mustard, pepper, lemon juice and vinegar to a bowl and slowly whisk in the oil – easy with the KitchenAid. Then stir through the spring onions and sour cream. I actually blanched the spring onions so they weren't overpowering – but you don't need to.

2 To make the chips, boil and drain the pinkeyes the cut into chips. First fry off the chorizo in a little oil and set aside. Then fry the chips in the same oil until golden. Remove chips and add the quinoa to the pan and fry until just coloured. Place the chips on a plate and top with chorizo and quinoa.

3 For the fish, mix the flour, pepper and salt. Cut the fins off the fish with scissors as they can burn depending on the size of the fish. Coat the fish in flour and deep fry until golden (about five minutes).

islandmenu.com.au

LEMON-CURD-FILLED DOUGHNUTS

Fresh lemons are in season right now and that makes me pretty excited, as they are one of my favourite flavours (along with basil, mint, vanilla ...) Sadly we don't have a fruit-producing lemon tree (yet) but luckily one of the ladies at work kindly brought in several bags of them from her tree and I scooped up quite a few for last weekend's cooking. I think they are Meyer lemons – they are almost orange in colour and so juicy.

So what to do with a load of lemons, besides lemonade (which I made this weekend as well, great with vodka)? Make lemon curd and pipe it into the middle of fluffy soft doughnuts, that's what!

The last time I made doughnuts they were yeast free, but I was feeling more confident this time around and wanted them to be lighter and fluffier. It takes a little time and the lemon curd is best made a day in advance, but well worth it I think. They are perfect for a grey afternoon tea treat.

To make the lemon curd

2	lemons – zested and juiced
80g	sugar
90g	butter
4	egg yolks (I used fresh ones from my uncle's chickens)

1 Put the lemon juice, zest, sugar and butter into a saucepan on low heat until the sugar and butter melt. Remove from the stove top.

2 In a separate bowl whisk the egg yolks, then add them to the saucepan and whisk vigorously. Return the pan to low heat and whisk continuously as the curd starts to thicken. Once the curd thickens, remove from the heat. Pass the curd through a sieve into a bowl then cover the curd directly with cling film and put in the fridge overnight.

To make the doughnuts I used a Donna Hay recipe and made them slightly larger so the mixture yielded 12. You will need to have the oil a bit cooler so they cook slower and right through.

Coat the warm doughnuts in sugar then fill a piping bag, with a small round nozzle, with the lemon curd.

HONEY GRAVLAX

Last week one of my mates let me know that some more Atlantic salmon had escaped down the Huon. This was far too tempting so I rescheduled a couple of meetings and we headed down for sunrise. It was a pretty productive morning, we ended up with two salmon and one trout.

Ingredients

2	fillets of Atlantic salmon – skin on and pin-boned
1	cup of honey at room temperature
3/4 cup	sea salt flakes
2 tbsp	cracked black pepper
1 cup	chopped basil

Method

1 In a large tray sprinkle a little of the sea salt over the bottom then lay the fillets skin side down. Evenly sprinkle the pepper, salt and honey over them – in that order. Then evenly place the basil over the fillets.

2 Take one fillet and turn it 180 degrees so it is facing the opposite way and place it on the other fillet skin side up.

3 Wrap in plastic wrap, then place a chopping board on top of the salmon with weights on top of the chopping board (cans of soup or beer work well).

4 Place in the fridge and leave for 24 hours and then turn. Put back in the fridge for another 24 hours. It should take about two days but keep an eye on it – it depends on the size of the fillets. You know it is done when the tail bits start to go a little rubbery.

5 Wash off all the salt and honey under fresh water, pat dry, add a little more pepper and pop it back in the fridge on a plate uncovered for about a day to dry it out a little – you could do it in a cool spot in the open instead.

To serve

My favorite thing in the world is gravlax and scrambled eggs. This time I crumbled some blue cheese in with the eggs – the sharpness of the cheese worked well with the honey. Alternatively serve the gravlax with a dill and lemon mayo and pickles on some crisp bread.

islandmenu.com.au

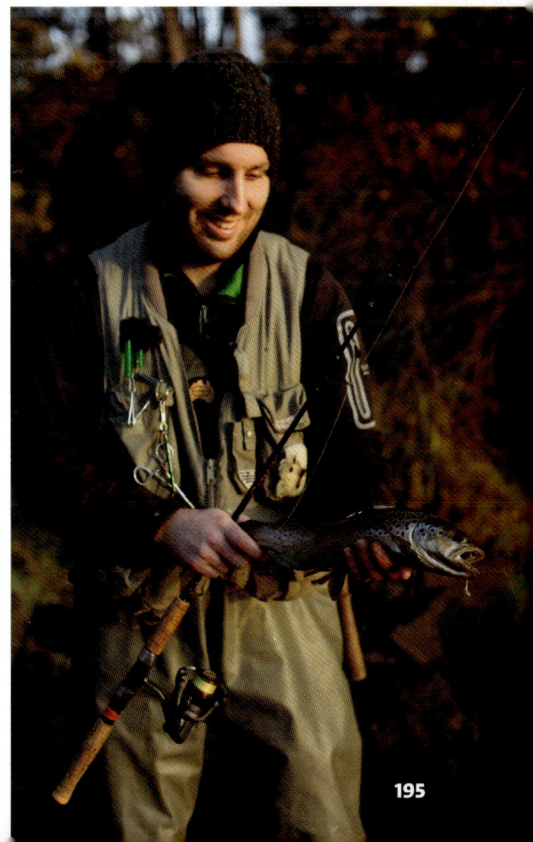

195

LAMB, BLUE CHEESE & HONEY SAUSAGES

These sausages would have to be my new favourite food; I call it a "Fancy Kransky". It took a while to get the mix right, because you can't really taste the mince as you go – well you could if you want I suppose – but it was worth a few failures.

This morning was perfect, so we cooked them on the rocks down the front of our place for breakfast. We served them with a fried egg and used the yolk as a sauce. They are fairly strong and it may be that not everyone wants to start the day this way, but you can always have them for tea. They are also the perfect hangover cure!

Ingredients

1kg (2.2 lbs)	fatty lamb off-cuts
200g (7 oz)	blue cheese chopped into half-centimetre cubes
2 tbsp	finely chopped rosemary
2 tbsp	honey
1 tbsp	Dijon mustard
3 tbsp	ice water
1m (~3 feet)	sausage skin
	Pepper and salt to season
1 twig	rosemary

Method

1 Mince the lamb (I used the mincing attachment for the KitchenAid). Mix in the honey, rosemary, pepper, salt, and mustard. Then fold through the cheese.

2 Chill the mince until it's quite cold, and then add the ice water. Thread the sausage skin onto you sausage maker (again, I used the sausage maker attachment for the KitchenAid). Tie a knot in the end. Put the mince through the sausage maker and make one continuous sausage.

3 Roll into spirals and spear with the rosemary to hold it together. This will make about two spirals. If you don't have a sausage maker, just make hamburgers out of them by adding an egg to the mix and rolling the patty in breadcrumbs.

4 Cook in a cast-iron skillet until cooked through and browned on the outside. Serve with eggs, sunny-side up, and toast.

islandmenu.com.au

STRIPEY TRUMPETER AND MUSHROOM PIE

Last week I had one of the best days fishing I have had for a long time. We left Hobart at 5am and launched the boat from Eaglehawk Neck for sunrise with tuna on our mind. The tuna weren't really on the chew as the weather was too nice – they love it in a dirty south-wester down there so we decided to give bottom fishing a bit of a crack. Long story short, we boated 12 stripey trumpeter in about an hour and a half. Most of the time was actually spent winding them up as we were in almost 200 metres of water. I had sore arms for days! There were even a couple of whales down there but the fishing was too good to go and take photos of them.

I would have to say tha stripey trumpeter would have to be my favorite eating fish, so I normally don't like doing too much to it. But in this case because we had a boatload of it I decided to try a few different recipes. Because it is autumn and there are mushrooms all over our front lawn this pie seemed to fit the bill nicely.

islandmenu.com.au

198

Ingredients

4	floury potatoes
1	egg
800g	stripey trumpeter, cubed
300ml	sour cream
	Zest of half a lemon
½	lemon, sliced thinly and quartered
2 punnets	mushroom – mix it up a bit by adding shitake, honey brown and oyster
3	shallots, sliced
3	bay leaves
1½ cm slice	speck
	White pepper and salt
1 cup	fish stock
	A few sprigs of rosemary
100g	butter

Method

1 Put the rosemary – just a little – and the shallots, butter, zest, speck, bay leaf, pepper, salt and mushroom in a pan on a low heat and soften.

2 Add the sour cream fish stock – you can add a splash of white wine if you want. Let this simmer and reduce a bit.

3 Boil the potatoes and put them through a ricer and allow to cool. Then add few tablespoons of butter and the egg and mix well.

4 In a decent pie dish cover the bottom with the fish and add the sauce. Make little dumplings out of the potatoes and place them on top of the fish and add a few lemon wedges.

5 Put in a hot-ish oven, say 200 degrees Celsius, and cook until the potato is golden.

The end

We hope you've found some treasures in these pages. If you'd like to find even more just head to **tailoredtasmania.com** for plenty more local secrets and up-to-the-minute snippets. We'll share them as we discover them so you can enjoy them too. You'll find us on social media as well, but mostly we spend our time out in the fresh air finding the latest fun to be had on our home turf. And, if you're ever wandering through Salamanca Market, come and say hello. We're just a few stalls up from Irish Murphy's (site 44) with plenty of books on hand. We're always happy to meet you.

Website tailoredtasmania.com
Facebook fb.com/tailoredtasmania
Instagram @tailoredtasmania
Twitter @tailoredtasmania
Email tailoredtasmania@gmail.com

Where do I begin with the thank you list for this book? For one I'd like to thank all the local businesses that you see spread across these pages. They took a leap of Tailored Tasmania faith by hopping aboard this book and you are the folk I celebrate and thank. Without your passion, the pages would be blank. Without your vision, Tassie would have slightly less sparkle. Each of you form the patchwork of the Tassie I love.

To Lea my designer, who was promised a 'small book on Tassie' and received an additional 5423 emails when I couldn't stop discovering new treasures, I thank you. Thank you for your patience, and your eye for beautiful design. As with all my books – I deliver you words and images, and you turn them into something beautiful. You're a joy to work with.

Bruce, my dear editor, without you my words would be a jumble, riddled with embarrassing typos. You've probably just corrected that sentence. I couldn't do my work without your watchful eye a few lines behind me.

To my family and my friends who shared their secrets and part of what makes home special to you, I am grateful. You make up the fabric of this book just as much as the landscape around me. I so appreciate your contribution. Those that are close to me, I thank you for putting up with my 3am writing sprees and quietly delivering me lunch in between madly typing.

To the photographers – you make this book come alive and it's been a pleasure meeting you all along the way and getting to know others of you better. You're a passionate bunch that encourage me to explore more. Sam Shelley, your Island Menu recipes are a rare treasure. Behind that casual manner of yours is a giftedness I've not seen. You capture Tassie in a way that reflects what you feel for it. Alice Gray, your skills behind a camera are only matched by your generosity. You are the definition of country hospitality and kindness. Andrew Wilson, your eye for detail has been a welcomed surprise as more of your work appeared across the pages.

And I thank all the people who are reading these words. Those who are here to discover Tasmania and those who call it home. It's such a special place and one that I share with a good dose of pride. I hope you find a new little discovery or two in these pages that seed a story of your own to keep.

Alice Hansen

Notes

Here are a couple of pages for you to write notes, journal or propose to someone in writing....

Image Credit & Location

Cover: Jam Jar Lounge (Alice Hansen)
P. 3 Mortimer Bay (3rd image – Kathryn Leahy)
P. 4-5 Island Menu (Sam Shelley)
P. 8-9 Battery Point (Alice Hansen)
P. 14 Mount Wellington sunrise (Alice Hansen)
P. 14 Christie Sweeting portrait (Alastair Bett)
P. 16 Masaaki – Farmers Market (Alice Hansen)
P. 21 Chris Hood in north east Tas (Vincent Pardieu)
P. 22-23 Oyster and Pearl (David Pyefinch)
P. 25 Bill Lark (courtesy of Lark Distillery)
P. 28-29 Gourmania (Sam Shelley)
P. 32-33 Zimmah (Andrew Wilson)
P. 36-37 Rebecca Roth (Amy Brown)
P. 42-43 Hobart Yachts – Tasman Peninsula (Jimmy Emms)
P. 48 + 49 Hobart Docks (Alice Hansen)
P. 50 + 51 Bruny Island (courtesy of TAA)
P. 52 + 53 Sandy Bay/River Derwent (courtesy of Wrest Point)
P. 60-62 100 Elizabeth St (Sarah Williams)
P. 66 Villino (Robert Karacic)
P. 67 Tasmanian Whisky Tours (Andrew Wilson)
P. 69 Norman & Dann (Peter Whyte)
P. 75 Pilgrim Coffee (Jess Reardon)
P. 79 Small Fry (Chris Young)
P. 80 Signal Station – Aerial Vision Australia
P. 83 Sixty Jazz Club (Eden Meure)

P. 85 Tasmanian Museum and Art Gallery (Francis Jones Morehen Thorp)
P. 87 Nick Randall Design (Peter Whyte)
P. 89 Art of Silver (Courtesy of TAOS)
P. 94 Cleburne Homestead (David Lander)
P. 95 55 Davey Accommodation (Dave Unwin)
P. 95 At Eleven Accommodation (Jonathan Jones)
P. 98 Pinnacle Mount Wellington (Alice Hansen)
P. 99 Secret Falls & Junction Hut (Alice Hansen)
P. 103 + 108 Two Metre Tall (Sam Shelley)
P. 110 You'll have to ask a local! (Alice Hansen)
P. 111 Cygnet (Alice Hansen)
P. 112 + 117 The Apple Shed (Jonathan Wherrett)
P. 113 The Apple Shed (Alice Hansen)
P. 122 Frogmore Creek Wines (Alice Hansen)
P. 127 Left: Adventure Bay (Alice Hansen)
P. 128-129 Satellite Island (Mark Chew)
P. 128-129 Satellite Island (Kara Rosenlund & Mark Chew)
P. 144 Belgrove Distillery (Kathleen Davies)
P. 149 Bangor (Alice Gray)
P. 150 Honeymoon Bay area (Alice Hansen)
P. 160 East Coast Cruises (Matt Davey)
P. 161 Dark Mofo (Alice Hansen)
P. 162 Dove Lake (Alice Hansen)
P. 170-197 Island Menu (Sam Shelley)